CAME *the* DAY

15

15

Above: Official photograph of Prisoners of War in Stalag XXB.
Right: Gren's metal dog tag, which says Prisoner of War (Kriegsgefangener) –
Camp (Lager), Thorn 7761. The tags were made so that upon a prisoner's release
they could be snapped in half, the Germans keeping one half and the Prisoner
retaining the other, to enable him to be identified when he returned to his own
country. They had to be worn around a prisoner's neck at all times.

CAME *the* DAY

EDITED BY JEAN SMITH

MEMOIRS OF KRIEGSGEFANGENER 7761

The reminiscences of Grenville John Davies, a World War II soldier, who endured approximately five years in Prisoner of War Work Camps followed by a long march through Poland and Germany.

BREWIN BOOKS

First published by
Brewin Books Ltd, 56 Alcester Road,
Studley, Warwickshire B80 7LG in 2007
www.brewinbooks.com

© Jean Smith 2007

ISBN: 978 1 85858 401 0

The moral right of the author has been asserted

A Cataloguing in Publication Record
for this title is available from the British Library

Typeset in Baskerville
Printed in Great Britain by
Cromwell Press Ltd.

CONTENTS

PREFACE   vi

1   MY EARLY YEARS IN SOUTH WALES   1

2   MOVE TO BIRMINGHAM   10

3   POSTING TO FRANCE   16

4   CAPTURE AND TRANSPORTATION   27

5   THORN – STALAG XXA   36

6   STALAG XXB – MARIENBURG – THE CAMP   53

7   FORCED LABOUR WORK PARTIES   66

8   TRIAL, RETRIBUTION AND THE REICHBAHN PARTY   81

9   SUGAR FACTORY   88

10 RETURN TO MARIENBURG   93

11 THE MARCH   101

12 RETURN JOURNEY   114

PREFACE

The reminiscences in this book, retold by Grenville (Gren) J. Davies, are taken from his original scrappy notes scribbled with the stub of a pencil on odd bits of paper he was able to acquire during his five years of captivity in Germany and Poland during World War II. By the time of retelling in 2004 these were becoming rather faded, and in danger of being lost.

I feel it has been a great privilege to simply be the tool, the means of putting into order and recording for posterity, what must be very painful memories from a wonderful gentleman who gave up five years of his youth to fight a war that has enabled my generation to live a happy, carefree, and basically affluent lifestyle.

Being born at the beginning of 1940 I remember very little about World War II, but as my own father was called up six months after my birth, for the first five years of my life I grew up without knowing him, a fact that was a very great grief to my father and subsequently to me also. Later in life my mother often recalled that when father came home on leave I burst into tears and refused to have anything to do with him which leaves no doubt whatsoever in my mind that because of this, for many years following his demob, we were unable to have a close relationship. Although the very best of friends, and I grew to love him dearly later in life, as a child I remember there always seemed to be a barrier between us and, although he was the mildest of men, I was rather frightened of him. For many years following the war, if I needed my father's permission for anything, I never felt able to ask him myself and requested my mother do it for me.

For the young men who survived the war this must have been the case in so many families and I feel we should be eternally grateful, and keep their sufferings very much in the public eye, as a tribute to, not only the horrors of war they experienced, but also to their loss of family life, which they willingly sacrificed to enable future generations to lead a comfortable and democratic lifestyle.

I personally feel Gren has glossed over what must have been a terrifying and totally horrific experience for five years of his young life. Having seen the anguish in his face at times when recalling his years as a POW I have no doubt there are many horrors hidden in the depths that he still cannot bear to relate, and, like so many of these brave young men, will never disclose to the world to help our understanding of what it was really like.

However, I have recounted his reminiscences, basically in his own words just as he related them to me, as a tribute to his bravery, and in the hope that they will never be allowed to die and will never be repeated.

I would like to thank Gren for agreeing to tell his story, my husband who has helped by recording hours of sessions of chat, supported the project whole heartedly and acted as proof reader and adviser, Helen and Stuart Mills for allowing me to use material and ideas from reminiscences of World War II recorded by their father and Barry Reid for allowing me to include a letter card and photograph of another prisoner held in Stalag XXA found in his mother's effects following her death.

Jean Smith

December 1939 – Private Grenville John Davies – 14th Army Field Workshop,
Royal Army Ordnance Corp. Just prior to being posted to France.

1

My Early Years In South Wales

I was born in Llanbradach which is situated in the mouth of the Rhymney Valley in South Wales, two and a half miles from Caerphilly, nine miles from Cardiff, and described in Kelly's Directory for 1914 as a mining village and ecclesiastical parish with a population (in 1911) of 4,998. The colliery provided employment for about 2,500 men and boys, most of whom lived in the village, while others walked or travelled by train from neighbouring villages and towns.

Gren & Jock.

My parents intended me to be named Grenville John Davies but when my father went to register my birth the Registrar, a somewhat dictatorial fellow, refused to register Grenville saying there was no such name, and insisted upon officially registering me as Granville. However, my parents always called me Grenville and that name has stayed with me.

My paternal grandfather, William Henry born in 1859, initially was a fireman in the local colliery, but when his son, Tom Henry, was seven months old his father's left arm was blown off below the elbow while attempting to "make a bang", a ruse suggested to him in honour of the pit manager's wedding day, by a couple of work-mates he met in the pub.

Mr & Mrs W. H. Davies.

Explosives they had stolen from the colliery detonated prematurely. The doctor was summoned, arrived from the next village by pony and trap and operated on William on his own kitchen table. Upon recovery he resumed work at the colliery where he progressed to Under-Manager, and following retirement lived to the ripe old age of seventy-nine.

When my maternal grandfather, who had cancer, knew that he was dying he decided to settle his wife in a business that she could manage herself. South Wales at that time was not a flourishing area but coal mining was a growing industry and grandfather, realising the need for substantial footwear for pit work, seized the opportunity to set up in business selling boots. He moved to South Wales but unfortunately was not there long before he died and was buried in Caerphilly church. My maternal grandmother, who was a remarkable woman, could not read or write, but could keep books. In her business she used hieroglyphics, which were perfectly understandable to her (i.e. a particular squiggle meant that Mrs Jones, 6 Garden Street, had left 6d deposit on a pair of shoes). She then translated the meaning to her daughters who entered a 'proper' copy in a ledger.

My parents were Beatrice May Crates, a highly respected dressmaker, and Tom Henry Davies, the only member of his family to be born in Llanbradach following his parents' move from further up the valley.

My mother was a Bristolian whose father, who died years before I was born, was a boot and shoe manufacturer. She came from a family of one boy and three girls, the boy being the eldest member of the family. As an extremely talented dressmaker she displayed her wares in grandmother's double fronted shop, which was in the centre of the village. Boots and

Left: Beatrice May Crates c. 1930.
Right: Tom Henry Davies. Photo sent to Gren in Stalag XXB in June 1944.

shoes were displayed in one window and the most elegant dresses in the other. She travelled up and down the valleys making dresses for many eminent people in the area. Mother's brother Jim, who couldn't abide runny noses, was known for frequently standing in the doorway of the shop when children were going to and from school. When a child came past with a runny nose he would disappear inside the shop and emerge a few moments later to present the child with a handkerchief. Next was Florence, known as Floss. She was a window-dresser working for some of the big stores in Cardiff, which in those days was a job to be proud of. My mother came next and then Ethel, the youngest, a music

Jim Crates killed in the Dardanelles.

teacher who taught piano and had a wonderful contralto voice. She was runner-up in the Welsh National Eisteddfod for a couple of years, ended up living in Evesham and ran the Evesham Ladies Choir.

Uncle Jim, a sniper in the army during the First World War, was sent to Gallipoli where, unfortunately, he was killed defending a rocky promontory. He was buried at sea and his name is inscribed on the cenotaph in Llanbradach. I was intrigued to find, during research to build a family tree, that Jim was shown as being married but living in Llanbradach whilst his wife and three children lived in Bristol. He was an entrepreneur and, I understand, bought an opencast coalmine in a village close to Llanbradach. He was a friend of Freddie Fox, an eminent jockey pre-Gordon Richards time, and even in later life, when I was a little boy, Freddie Fox still kept in touch with Jim's wife to give her racing tips, which she then passed on to my grandmother to enable her to have a little flutter. Sadly, later in life grandmother tended to get confused about the messages and I remember on one occasion, when she had been told to back a horse called Counterpane, she unfortunately missed boosting her income by looking for a horse called Eiderdown!

Father was born, bred and died in Llanbradach and was the youngest member of five children, the others being girls. His name was Tom Henry – not Thomas or Tommy. If anyone called asking if Tommy was coming out to play my grandmother would say "He's not Tommy, he's Tom Henry" and she always referred to him as Tom Henry for the rest of her life. He began work when he was fourteen on the 'Screens'. These were moving belts along which the coal was transported on trays and the youngsters picked out any stones or slate from amongst the coal. At the age of sixteen he went to work underground where there were more than 300 pit ponies in use, his weekly wage being two shillings

Gren aged 12 years.

and sixpence (12½p). Two stories I clearly remember my father telling me were firstly that every payday (pay being in cash), when the siblings came home, his mother sat with her 'pinny' held out into which each of them had to tip their earnings. My grandmother then handed sixpence (2½p) back for use as pocket money. Secondly the headmaster of the local school, T.P. Davies noticed one day that as he passed a pupil on the way to school he did not touch his cap. Later the boy was summoned to the headmaster's study where he was given a sound thrashing for his lack of respect.

My dad had been educated at the "National School for promoting the Education of the Poor in the Principles of the Established Church throughout England and Wales" – known locally as "The Church School". "Managers", who were not elected by the public, controlled these "National" schools, founded by endowment or subscription and maintained partly from this source and partly by Government grants, but not by rates. Under the provision of the Education Act of 1870, the Eglwysilan School Board was established. This Act imposed the duty of providing an elementary education for children in their area upon all boroughs and parishes, and on 10th September 1900 the Coedybrain

Mixed and Infants Schools, built by the Eglwysilan School Board, welcomed its first pupils. That is where I began my education, later moving to Caerphilly Secondary School (as it was known in those pre-Grammar school days).

The Civil Parish Eglwysilan School Board was in existence for approximately thirty-two years as the Education Act of 1902 abolished all School Boards and transferred their responsibilities to County Councils who were already providing intermediate (or secondary) education. This meant that the Board Schools at Coedybrain and neighbouring Castell Coch were the last to be opened under the old system.

Dad had four sisters, two nice ones Edith Jane, and Jemima who died early from Tuberculosis which was very prevalent in those days, and Emily and Ethel who rather resented my parents' marriage. Emily married, though I never saw her husband; apparently he attempted suicide on two occasions and was referred to a mental home. They had a son slightly younger than me. Ethel remained single until her fifties when she eventually married her cousin Ludwig Thomas. Some years later, when dad and I were tending mother's grave we noticed the grave of Ethel's husband. Each time we visited the cemetery dad wondered what had happened to Aunt Ethel, and where she was buried, as he felt sure she must be dead by then. It was not until many years later, and several years after my father had died, whilst tending his grave I noticed that the stone to the grave of Aunt Ethel's husband had been removed and a mound of new soil now covered the grave topped by a few dead wreaths. The next time I visited the headstone had been re-erected and on it had been added, "And his wife, Ethel aged 102". This caused me considerable amusement as dad had had her buried in that graveyard for the past forty or so years!

Like most of the men and boys of the village, father initially worked as a collier until enlisting in the Irish Rifles in 1914. He later transferred to the Royal Engineers and was promoted to Sergeant. After being demobbed, instead of going back down the pit, he went to work at the colliery by-products plant where they made coke, naphthalene and various other by-products from the coal. It was very hard work and the wages were a pittance. I never remember my father handling any money for, as in his

Left: July 1946 Colin Derek Stuart Davies who served in Palestine.
Right: The wedding of Beatrice May Crates to Thomas Henry Davies 3rd
September 1918. On the bride's left Ethel Crates (Music Teacher) and kneeling in
front of her Edna Crates (the bride's niece).

early days with my grandmother, he immediately handed over his wages to mother as soon as he arrived home on payday. She was a wonderful manager who sensed when things needed doing and consequently my father, who'd never had to buy *anything*, was completely lost when she died.

Following my parents' marriage on 3rd September 1918 I was born on 15th September 1919 and my brother Colin Derek Stuart (known as Derek) followed in 1927. Immediately after the First World War, when houses were at a premium, we shared a house with another family, later moving to live with my father's sister until the glorious day, when I was about three years old, we eventually moved to a house of our own in Church Street, later undertaking our final move to Garden Street.

During my childhood life in the village was happy and carefree if somewhat hard, and although we were not well off mother, who was able to supplement our income with her dressmaking, managed the housekeeping well. We led a comfortable existence and never went short of food.

Unfortunately mother died in 1937 at the very young age of forty-two leaving father to bring up a teenager and ten year old lad. Father re-married in 1939 and my half brother, Anthony Ross, (who accompanied me on my return trip to retrace the march in 2000), was born when I was home on leave in January 1946. Sadly dad's second wife then, very unexpectedly, died when Anthony was only four. Some years later dad married again, but even his third wife pre-deceased him, following which he spent the remainder of his life alone in his Garden Street house until he died at the ripe old age of ninety-two.

When a funeral took place in the village, no one used a hearse. The coffin was carried by relays of four men, from the house of mourning to the local cemetery, a journey of approximately two miles, the mourners, including women and children, walking behind dressed in black.

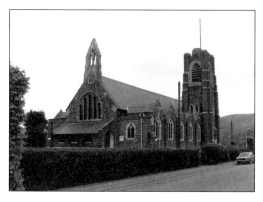

Interior and exterior views of The Church of Wales in Llanbradach, where Gren was a choirboy. Gren's father's was the last funeral to be conducted in the church before it was demolished.

There was an abundance of chapels in Llanbradach village and a Church of Wales, (the Welsh equivalent of the Church of England), a lovely church which sadly was demolished a few years ago due to subsidence from the colliery workings.

Originally I attended the Sion church, which was a Welsh Chapel. I could not speak Welsh, but the children next door attended and decided to take me to Sunday School with them. Around the same time my

Gren aged 9 and a half years.

maternal grandmother, who attended the Church of Wales, took me along to services with her. I was fascinated with the choirboys in their cassocks and surplices, and when I was about nine and a half years old decided to join the choir. From then on I became addicted to the church and when my voice broke became a Server, regularly attending three times on Sundays and the Wednesday evening service as well. Therefore, when I came to Birmingham the natural thing for me to do was to join a church.

2

Move To Birmingham

I came to Birmingham in 1935, aged sixteen, to spend a short holiday with my mother's sister who lived in Rubery, a suburb of the City. At first I joined St. Chad's but, as this was very High Church where incense was swung, felt it was not for me, so transferred to the Congregational Church in Whetty Lane, Rubery, where I was very happy and got on really well with the people.

Shortly after my arrival in Birmingham, I began to feel restless and a need to move on from school, so I enquired about a job at the Austin Motor Works where they agreed to take me on as a Stores Assistant.

Upon starting work I initially moved into a bed-sitter in a family home in Rubery then, after twelve months, moved to a home where the landlady was a widow with a son seven years older than me. She was a motherly type who laid the law down from the beginning insisting I was in by 9.30pm on weekdays and 10pm at weekends. Having been proud possessor of 'the key of the door' at my previous accommodation, being dictated to as to what time I should be in at night did not go down well and I decided there and then I would not be staying long. However, I came to appreciate her care and concern and what she did for me and my stay became very lengthy, during which time I formed many friendships with local lads.

I had taken the step of leaving school on my own initiative and without consulting anyone, which caused some considerable concern to my father. He decided to visit Birmingham and speak to someone at the Austin who told him they were just about to start a Trade Apprenticeship scheme and it seemed that, because of my 'Secondary School' education, I had the necessary background and qualifications to fit the criteria. Therefore, I progressed from being a Stores Assistant to becoming one of the Austin's first Trade Apprentices.

In 1937 Rubery was a very small village and the only entertainment available was a Saturday night concert in the Congregational church hall, known as 'The Popular Saturday Night Concert', where local talent provided the entertainment. One of the main regular attractions was Betty Fox's School of Dance. There being little for local youths to do we approached the church authorities with a request to start a Youth Club. This began in a small way, somebody bringing a dartboard, someone else a ring board and I provided a set of boxing gloves, which had been bought for me, by my father, when I was a very young lad. Father was quite an athletic man, and both a very good footballer and boxer. His greatest pleasure in life was to attend boxing matches and his main ambition for me was that I should become heavyweight champion of the world. Unfortunately, as far as this hope went, and much to his disappointment, I did not attain to his aspirations! Mother always knew when a big fight was coming to Cardiff and saved sufficient money to enable father to attend plus £1 for a bet. He was incredibly adept at assessing the outcome and always came home with more money than he took. At the Youth Club we used trestle tables for table tennis, and also formed a football team, which was horrendous for the first year. Even I turned out and I was a hopeless player, but the following year several other chaps joined, the team improved greatly, and we actually won the Kings Norton Cup.

Next a Dramatic Society was formed which my pals wanted to join but I had no inclination to belong to anything like that. However, I was pretty handy at carpentry and used to enjoy doing woodwork, so my landlady's son, Jack, and I agreed to go along to help make the scenery. To whet people's appetite the group first put on a little one-act play, which proved to be a great success. At the next meeting auditions were to take place to cast *The Farmer's Wife* by Eden Philpot. The prospective candidates were ushered into a room to be called forth for their auditions and Jack and I sat down to await the outcome. The producer, Cyril Thornton, said, "Come on – in the other room". "Oh no," we said, "we only want to make scenery". However, he insisted we audition and Jack and I ended up with the two juvenile leads, much to the annoyance of my pals who were the ones initially interested and who now only had 'bit' parts. We put on one or two more plays and then I was given a leading role in *The Strange Case of Blondie White*, which we were scheduled to perform at the end of September 1939. However, this was not to be as world events overtook us and war broke out.

That was my initiation into amateur dramatics, an interest that has remained with me to the present day, and formed a large part of my life. After the war I produced many local productions for the Allens' Cross Community Players, and, in 1961, with a production of *Save the Standard*, we gained first place in Birmingham and second place in Hereford Midland Divisional Finals.

This qualified the Players to appear in the British Drama League's Western Area Final where the Adjudicator, Cecil Bellamy, was 'much impressed' by our performance.

Gren being presented with the award by Bernard Hepton, third from left, in 1961.

Hostilities had been looming on the horizon since 1936 with Germany "Annexing" adjacent countries, therefore, in 1938 when war was pre-eminent following Neville Chamberlain's return from Germany, there was general upheaval and all the apprentices at the Austin Works were deputed to fill sand bags as a precautionary measure, a task which I seem to remember lasted two whole days.

Before long we were all instructed to attend a meeting, commissioned by the head of the Apprentices' Department who, having recently become involved with the Territorial Army, had started a recruiting campaign for the Army Service Corps amongst the apprentices at the Austin. From the Authority's point of view, it was now preferable to persuade chaps initially to join the TA and at this meeting Officers of the Territorial Army explained what was involved and told us what a good thing it would be if we joined. At this stage the UK Government found that, whereas the naval force was of reasonable strength, the land forces and airforce were virtually non-existent. A massive re-armament programme was launched and on 26th April 1939 conscription into the Militia was introduced. Upon reaching the age of 21 Military Service was now compulsory for six months, followed by eighteen months on the reserve or in the TA. The minimum age for Military Service was twenty years, but a proviso was now added stating that those who joined the TA before a specific date would be exempt from conscription into the Militia. As time went by we still believed hostilities would just fritter out and a friend and I decided that when we finished our apprenticeships we would go to America. However, the situation began to get far more serious and the outbreak of war became increasingly imminent. By the time the recruiting campaign took place at the Austin, it had been announced that for those joining the Territorials before a certain deadline Militia service would be waived. All eligible men were encouraged to sign up which resulted in a large percentage of apprentices joining the regular established TA unit based in Harborne, but I didn't feel this was for me. Before long another directive came through declaring that all service in the TA prior to conscription into the Militia, would be deducted from the eighteen months TA service following Militia training. This new directive gave me the idea that as I was nineteen I would be able to do my eighteen months training before I finished my

Apprenticeship at twenty-one then we could still go to America, and so, after some discussion, three friends, Francis Hill, Norman Blunn, Wilfred Jackson and I decided, as we didn't fancy being recruited into the Militia as green, raw recruits, we would join the TA. Francis, who owned an Austin Big 7, bundled us all into his car one evening and we went to join the Service Corps at Harborne. They were not taking more recruits at that time but sent us to join the Military Police. They only wanted motorcyclists so we then went to Hall Green to join the Signal Corps. They too were full up so we thought, "Forget it", and went back home.

Every week at the Austin an Apprentices' Bulletin was issued and some weeks later it mentioned that a Mr. Prestage, who was the Vauxhall dealer in the Horsefair in Birmingham, was contemplating starting a completely new TA Unit of the Royal Army Ordnance Corps and asked for anyone interested to contact him. I wrote on behalf of my friends and received a reply to the effect that there was sufficient interest to start a unit, so on 29th July 1939, we all went to sign up at a type of warehouse in Tyburn Road which turned out to be our H.Q. for the next few months. No uniforms were available, but we practised once a week incessant marching back and forth. Came the 1st September, the Friday prior to war breaking out on Sunday 3rd, when, to comply with blackout regulations, most of the apprentices had been employed for a couple of days in painting the fanlights on top of the factory building with black paint. I came down from doing this job sometime in the afternoon to be greeted by my pal who said, "I've been looking for you everywhere. A general 'Call Up' message has been issued and you've got to report to the Territorials". I went to the apprentices' office to find out whether this was so only to discover that everyone else had already gone. I was the last apprentice to leave and they were waiting for me to start the war! I met up with my other pals, and we all trooped off to Headquarters. So, at nineteen years of age, my war experience began and I served my six years throughout the war as a Territorial. We still hadn't any uniforms or weapons but spent all our time marching up and down. On the Sunday morning we were all gathered around the radio when war was declared – now the serious stuff was to begin – but I still kept my digs at Rubery, convinced it would all be over in a few weeks time.

Incidentally the first intake of conscripts were known as 'Belisha Boys' as the Minister of War at the time was Hoare Belisha, the same man who, as Minister of Transport, left his mark all over the UK with 'Belisha Crossings'.

There was no accommodation at Headquarters so, apart from one or two who stayed to look after the premises, or perform guard duty (despite the fact there was nothing to guard) we all went home at night. By this time several hundred young men had joined up and items of uniform were beginning to filter through in dribs and drabs. One day we were all issued with a cap each, perhaps a week later a shirt each and so on. We were split into two sections, the 14th Army Field Workshop, which was the section I was in and which turned out to be the biggest field workshop in the British Army when we were in France, and 5th Ordnance Field Park, a Supply Unit that was like a stores park. Eventually we divided and we never saw 5th Ordnance Field Park again. Time drifted on with us still going home at night and returning in the morning when we trained and paraded in our civilian clothes. Gradually more items of uniform began to come through and we were given an allowance of 2/- (10p) a week. It now became obvious we needed accommodation so we were moved to wooden huts, which had been built along the Bristol Road for use as temporary classrooms by King Edwards Grammar School. At this stage the Unit was constantly being strengthened by increasing numbers as Militiamen and Reservists (older TA men and ex-regular soldiers) joined us. The half of the buildings nearest to the Gun Barrels Pub was for the Army Field Workshop and the other half was for Ordnance Field Park use. I don't know where OFP went but eventually it was decided to move AFW to the military establishment at Aldershot, which made us realise things were becoming far more serious. As it was now obvious that I could no longer keep on my digs in Rubery, I was given a weekend leave to tidy up my affairs and arrange for my belongings to be moved back home to South Wales.

3

Posting To France

Upon moving to the military establishment at Aldershot we joined forces with 'real' soldiers, which was extremely embarrassing as we were so raw and terrible at everything we did. Our Sergeant Major, Charlie Ashford, had been a soldier in the First World War but was now employed by Birmingham City Council as a dustman. He resented intelligence, but could empty dustbins. He could drill extremely well and use a shovel, a fact of which he was very proud as picking up a shovel one day when we were trying to clear snow away he said, "I'll show you – this is how you use a bloody shovel". He came to France with us but the army failed to classify him as a tradesman of any description. They gave him an appointment as a clerk, at which he was hopeless; they tried him as a driver – he couldn't cope with that either, so in desperation they sent him back home where I believe he became a Drill Instructor. Anyway we never saw him again which was just as well as he still believed war consisted of bayonets and charging and he would undoubtedly have got us all killed.

Whilst in Aldershot we joined with other soldiers and Military Police and although we now had uniforms we still lacked various items of kit e.g. initially we didn't have respirators, (though these were issued to us later). Our civilian gas masks were in cardboard boxes and by this time had to accompany us everywhere we went. Consequently the boxes became very ripped and battered. Chaps whose boxes had broken wrapped their gas masks in brown paper; the posher ones amongst us having theirs in a little Rexine box. These were soldiers going out to fight the Germans, I ask you! When going out in the evening we donned our greatcoat pushing our gas mask into the pocket. The Redcaps used to get extremely annoyed. They'd stop us and demand, "Where's your respirator?" We'd reply, "We haven't got a respirator, we've only got a gas mask" and pull a bit of rubber out of our pocket. Talk about Fred Karno's Army! One day, whilst out on the big square performing our usual 'Square bashing', one of the highlights of being at Aldershot took place. A Canadian contingent arrived who were well equipped, fully kitted out and had a full complement of vehicles. They stood around the parade ground watching us perform. Charlie Ashford, who was taking the parade as usual, had a sudden inspiration. He shouted, "Gas". We all knew that if this was ever shouted gas masks had to be donned immediately. The Canadians fell about laughing at the scene that ensued, all the British soldiers pulling bits of rubber from their pockets, some untying bits of string, which was the only bit they had so it had to be carefully folded and returned to their pocket, others undoing their brown paper parcels. Obviously had there been a gas attack we would all have been dead long before our masks were prepared, let alone put on. It must have been November/December time before we were equipped with a full complement of kit, uniform, respirator and weapon.

Whilst at Aldershot we had drilled incessantly and gone to lectures where I saw an Anti Tank Rifle and a Bren gun, which was very useful as later I was made a Bren Gunner. We went to workshops in Aldershot *once* to do a trade test. Otherwise our time was spent with Charlie's incessant 'Square bashing', purgatory for one or two who could not get the correct rhythm for arms and legs. Admittedly Charlie could do it well and knew all the drill with all the fancy patterns but one questioned its usefulness in training us for war.

One member of our Unit was a tall gangling Australian by the name of Gates. I don't remember his christian name but he had worked for GEC in Birmingham, had been in the TA with me and we became quite friendly. Unfortunately he was always out of step and could not march in time so they made him a Lance Corporal and put him in charge of the Orderly Office. For the first time ever things ran efficiently. All orders, instructions and lists of guard duty etc. were regularly posted so that we all knew where we should be at any given time. Prior to Gates being appointed somebody was always running about at the last minute grabbing the nearest recruit to be 'on guard' because they'd forgotten to draw up a roster. I was out in Aldershot with him one day when a lorry came along and he said, "Let's go somewhere shall we?" I said, "Where?" "Oh I don't know," he said, and stopped the lorry. We jumped on the back and the driver asked where we wanted to go. Gates told him, "Wherever you're going will suit us fine", so we ended up in Guildford. I said, "You took a chance didn't you?" "Well, that's all right isn't it", Gates replied, "We're going somewhere". Then he asked if I would like to go to Australia. I said, "Yes but I don't suppose I ever will". "No", he said, "You won't, that's the difference between you and me. I wanted to come to England so I packed my bags and came"; and for him it was as simple as that. He was sent for a trade test, and if I remember correctly, upon his return had been promoted from Lance Corporal to First Class Warrant Officer. He knew more about electrics than the people who were testing him. When we went to France he was made Billeting Officer and wanted me to transfer as an electrician to be his Deputy Billeting Officer. Unfortunately, as he had been so anxious for me to be with him, this didn't happen, and I heard afterwards that he got back from France and ended up as a General. I've often wondered whether this was true.

Initially the first few months of war in this country were very quiet. The Germans vanquished Poland and Belgium, attacked the Scandinavian countries and with little apparent trouble began quite soon to march through France. Eventually we left Aldershot and went to a little place called Crondal just outside Farnham from where, as a member of the British Expeditionary Force, I was shipped to France on 29th December 1939 as a Private of the 14th A.F.W. R.A.O.C.

Gren looking sorry for himself having just received a TB jab prior to his posting to France.

The ship I travelled on was the Isle of Man Steam Packet, Mona's Queen, which subsequently, on 26th May 1940, took 1,420 men home from Dunkirk but was sunk three days later. The day preceding our sailing from Southampton to Cherbourg, I was promoted to Bren Gunner. The evening before we sailed my special pal Norman, who I first met whilst in Rubery, developed German measles and had to stay behind. He vowed that he would catch up with me when he recovered, but never did and I didn't see him again until after the war. He went through Africa and Italy, eventually married an Italian girl, and only died a few years ago. As both he and another chap, who was also a Bren Gunner, were taken ill, a strong chap was needed to carry the gun and ammunition and it was my misfortune to be standing in the wrong place at the wrong time. I was handed two big pouches with ammunition and told I was No. 2 on the Bren gun. In those days it took two men – one to load and one to fire the gun. I assumed my No. 1 knew how to fire the thing, as I didn't receive any instruction at all about its use. By this time we had all been issued with rifles and twenty rounds of ammunition, which I had to carry in addition to the ammunition for the Bren gun, all of which was extremely heavy and uncomfortable. I padded my shoulders with dusters to prevent my collar-bone from becoming raw where the ammunition clip dug in. With a British-made rifle slung over your shoulder the ammunition clip dug into your back whereas the German rifles were of a far superior design with the clip the other way round pointing away from the body. Our Unit was intended to be right at the rear carrying out repairs, and virtually non-combatant, therefore we did not receive any tuition at all as to how to fire any gun. But, in true Services' fashion, when we boarded the Mona's Queen for some reason or other, despite Infantry people being on board, we were given the dubious honour of manning the guns and our Adjutant was made Ship's Adjutant for the duration of the crossing. We stood the Bren gun on its stand on a large coil of rope, which was at the rear of the ship. We then had to climb over the rope to get inside for our periods of duty, which were two hours on and two hours off. It took us twenty-four hours to cross to Cherbourg, as we had to stop and wait numerous times, rumours being rife that there were U-Boats in the vicinity. Only expecting a short trip across the water no official rations had been issued, therefore we had no food at all on the journey. I was off duty when we arrived, and as I walked round the ship I passed a rail with half the ship's company hanging over it 'throwing up'. Up until that point I'd had no feelings of seasickness whatsoever, but witnessing the others being so ill encouraged me to join them. We alighted from the ship and were told food was available at the far end of the jetty. This turned out to be a large cauldron of the most revolting looking stewy stuff, which was a yellowish colour. Everyone refused it as they were convinced it had been collected on the way over! Later, having recovered a little, we eventually managed to buy some food from a canteen on the railway station.

It was late evening and pitch black by the time we all boarded a train for the next leg of our journey. Most of the fellows were simply herded into any of the carriages but one advantage of being a Bren Gunner was having a special compartment reserved for our use. Eight of us piled in and, as the Officers came along looking for space, in order to keep the compartment to ourselves and get a little peace and rest, we crowded the window to give the impression of the carriage being full. At this stage food was distributed and we received a twenty-four hours allocation of rations for a full compartment, which should have contained approximately twice as many men as were actually occupying ours. One of the items we were issued with was a 14lb tin of Bully Beef which we were told had to last us for two days, but as we had already eaten, our tin wasn't opened. After only a few hours' journey, upon arriving at our destination somewhere out in the wilds, we were told to take any remaining rations down to the front of the train to be collected. There was much chuntering to the effect that no one had any intention of carting these ruddy great tins around and they were surreptitiously deposited beneath the train. Having reached the place where we were to stay for a short while, which was only a little country village, we found the Advance Party there were starving. There were no shops and the local produce, which consisted primarily of eggs, had already been consumed so the first thing the Advance Party asked us for was food. With extreme feelings of guilt it was arranged for a truck to be sent, without delay, back to the railway siding to recover all the food we had thrown away.

In this village we witnessed the wonderful sight of trees festooned with mistletoe, which was the first time I had ever seen the parasite actually growing on trees. It was a bitterly cold winter with heavy snow and frost and we all had to sleep in a barn, which originally had double doors but had since lost one. The barn was adjacent to a cottage in which a farm labourer lived and outside which he had built a great wall of logs for his stock of winter fuel. He gave us permission to use some of the logs for a fire to keep us warm, but because it was so bitter in the barn during our stay we burned the lot. However, he was well reimbursed for his kindness and appeared totally satisfied.

We stayed there for a short while, and to fill in our time and help keep us warm, we were made to practise a great game of pretence at combat firing. Without any actual rounds ever being fired, one small group advanced whilst another gave them covering fire, then another group advanced under covering fire from the first group; and so it continued daily until one day when the Colonel came to see us. At a certain point the Sergeant Major announced, "When I blow my whistle all get up and charge with a blood curdling yell". By this time the chaps had endured enough of these stupid games of pretence, so when the whistle sounded, we charged forward and to a man yelled, "Up Your Pipe", an expression that was in very common use at the time. Amazingly there were no repercussions from our insubordination.

The day before we were due to move on, I succumbed to influenza and was extremely unwell. This had its advantageous side as the following day, upon reporting to the Sergeant that I was not well, he delegated someone else to carry the Bren gun ammunition.

We moved on to Hesdigneul-lès-Béthune, a coal mining area, where I was appointed Assistant Billeting Officer. From here we amused ourselves by visiting the towns of Béthune and Bruay to watch the nightlife in the brothels, and I can assure my readers it *was* only WATCHING! As Assistant Billeting Officer it was my responsibility to find accommodation for the unit with the local villagers. Some of the men slept in multiple accommodation such as store-houses but a few select people lived in private accommodation, and a friend and I went to live with an elderly couple where we had beds, a great luxury as this was the first time we had slept in a bed since leaving home, night-time always having been spent on the floor. We made ourselves at home for a few more weeks and set up a canteen and a boxing ring in some disused premises.

Going back to our Aldershot days where we ate in vast canteens, I'd had trouble with a chap named Woods who, one day, insisted on sitting in a seat I was saving for my mate Jackson. I became extremely annoyed with him and reported him to the Corporal, who ordered him away. Later on he came back to me and asked what room I was in. Naturally I refused to tell him but somehow he found out and informed me that he would bring the 'bits of leather' around that night. This was the first time I had heard this expression, but later discovered it was his terminology for 'Boxing Gloves'. He informed me he would be round at seven o'clock. I had sparred a bit in my time when I first came to Birmingham and still had the kit, black shorts with an amber stripe down the sides and boxing gloves given to me by my father, but I certainly did not class myself as a boxer. However, I donned my kit and, together with all the chaps in my room, waited, quivering and quaking, for the big fight to begin. Seven o'clock came with no sign of Woods, so after waiting the minimum amount of time, and as I was not anxious to be beaten to a pulp, I changed and we went into Aldershot. The following morning he sidled up to me on parade and told me, "Somebody had the 'bits of leather', so I wasn't able to come". Naturally I told him how very disappointed I was hoping desperately that the relief at his failure to turn up didn't show on my face, and felt I'd had a lucky escape, as he would probably have killed me. I had heard the rumour that he was a sparring partner to Peter Kane, a British champion boxer at that time, but it was obvious we both took a distinct dislike to each other.

Anyway, when we got to Hesdigneul and set up the boxing ring, Ted Yeo, a Londoner who was a professional fighter, took charge and proceeded to show some of the fellows all the dirty tricks he knew. One evening I was sitting watching the lads sparring with each other when Woods jumped into the ring. Ted asked who would give Woods a fight. His reputation as a boxer having preceded him there were no takers. Ted's eyes lighted on me and I was nominated to take him on. Not wishing to appear a 'chicken' I entered the ring. We had a few rounds stabbing at each other and all ended in a reasonably friendly fashion. Lo and behold, a few days later on the board appeared a notice advertising a Grand Boxing Tournament amongst which were the participants Woods v Davies. I protested vehemently but Ted insisted, "You did all right the other night", so I was put into the ring again. It was a three-round contest and in the first round Woods was hitting me all over the place. When I struggled back to my corner my second said, "Don't stand back, get in a bit sharpish this time", so deciding I had nothing to lose I dashed out when the bell rang and hit him. He was so stunned he wobbled into the corner from where I refused to let him emerge and kept on landing the punches. Eventually I won the fight and was presented with a packet of cigarettes and a few francs as my prize. He came to see me sometime later explaining I had been extremely lucky as he'd had a big meal before the fight and wasn't up to his usual standard, so to appease him I gave him my packet of cigarettes.

Next door to the elderly couple with whom I billeted lived a girl who was about our age, and the chap who billeted with me fell in love with her. The dilemma was he couldn't speak French and she couldn't speak English. I knew a modicum of schoolboy French and was enlisted to speak for him and interpret during their courting sessions, even though I could not understand the majority of what she was saying. However, he was genuinely in love with her and had every intention of returning to marry her when the war ended, but unfortunately he was killed.

Our next destination was a little town called Carvin, near Lille, where, on arrival, all the ordinary ranks were billeted in a two-storey disused bakery in the High Street. Again we were back to sleeping on the floor, which in this building was concrete. Across the road from our billet was a café with two petrol pumps on the forecourt, run by two young women whose husbands were fighting on the Maginot Line where the soldiers were very poorly paid. During our first few days in this area a small group of us visited the café regularly for food and drink, but not being too keen on French food we persuaded the girls to cook us egg and chips, which from then on became a firm favourite and helped turn their business into a thriving concern.

I was a keen Table-Tennis player, and was delighted to find a table in their garage, which adjoined the café. After setting it up we spent our off duty periods playing Table Tennis followed by a meal of egg and chips

Fitters Section, 14th Army Field Workshop, RAOC, March/April 1940 at Carvin.
Gren second row from front second in from right, Corporal Stewart Evans
(known as Bill) front row right.

together with a drink – absolute bliss! Soon the majority of the chaps in the unit began to patronise the café, and when they were extra busy I helped by serving behind the bar. I had no idea what the price of drinks was in France so simply charged a standard rate for all.

At the two previous places where we had stayed we carried out running repairs to vehicles and machinery, but at Carvin a fully equipped operational workshop was set up in premises down the road from our billet. We were split into four groups. I worked in Main Shops, the headquarters and remotest from any danger, the other three groups being Recoveries, which, in theory, were all nearer to the front line. They were smaller groups and carried out work on the spot, but any jobs that were too big for them to cope with were sent back to Main Shops where we had bigger and better facilities. Each day we went to the workshop to carry out repairs to the variety of army equipment sent to us – lorries, Bren gun carriers, tanks and various armoured vehicles. This continued until around mid-May when we were confined to barracks, instructed to load all the equipment into the wagons and pack our kit so that when the order came through we were ready to move out at a moment's notice. Whilst confined to barracks to our delight the girls from the café collected our orders for egg and chips, which they then delivered to us. After four days of mooning around we received instructions saying we were to be moved from our camp. Our officers were in private accommodation with their Mess adjacent to a brothel, and it was following a bomb dropped by a German plane, which, incidentally, just happened to blow up the brothel, that we received the *official* order to move out. Presumably the Officers decided there was little point in staying any longer! On my return, sixty years later, the area had been virtually re-built so I assume more bombing took place after we left.

We were now moved a short distance to a field in the grounds of a chateau. The vehicles were all placed around the perimeter of the field prior to our being called on parade where Colonel Prestage read out a signal he had received from General Gort congratulating us on our work and achievements to date and telling us we were being rewarded with a well-earned rest. We settled ourselves in to enjoy our rest when, to our horror, that evening enemy planes appeared on the scene and proceeded to bomb an airfield, which, unbeknown to us, was adjacent to our 'haven of rest'!

Obviously it was too dangerous to stay there any longer so, when dawn broke on 23rd May 1940, we were again on the move to another chateau within the locality of Audruicq about nineteen kilometres south east of Calais, where we duly waited for some German tanks to arrive and inflict considerable damage on us without any harm to them whatsoever! When this happened a group of us were some distance away having been sent down a large field on reconnaissance to see what we could find. Not seeing anything untoward we returned only to be severely reprimanded and told to "Get the hell back down there again and keep observing". As we went back we spotted German tanks making their way round to the rear of our unit. We turned round to find that all hell was being let loose back at camp where the majority of our chaps were. As we rushed back we ran into trucks that were evacuating the lads and by the time we reached camp the firing and shelling had virtually ended. The first truck we met stopped but was full up. We asked what was going on to be told that the Colonel had been out to see us, decided our position was hopeless, suggested we all tried to make our way to the coast, declared "Every man for himself", and wished us all good luck. Sadly we learned later that the Colonel and Lieutenant Austin were apparently making their get-away in a car when the car was fired on by 'friendly fire', French machine gunners who were supposed to be assisting us. Being a non-combatant unit, we had nothing to fight with so when Colonel Prestage realised our position was hopeless he contacted the French military to send assistance. The French came, set up a machine gun and decided they were going to shoot anything that came down that road. Unfortunately the next vehicle to traverse the road was the car carrying the Colonel and Lieutenant, which came in their direct line of fire, and they were both killed. That was the day we had our bit of action, in and out with a short, sharp push and never a round fired!

Four days later, on 27th May 1940, I was captured by the Germans.

4

CAPTURE AND TRANSPORTATION

The first truck we met went on ahead, I jumped in the second and, as I thought, fortunately got in with the driver. We were following the first truck, which came to a T-junction and turned in the direction of the tanks we had seen when on reconnaissance. Upon reaching the junction our driver began to turn right whereupon I said, "Don't go that way, we've just come from there where we found German tanks mustering". We went the other way and it wasn't until years later we heard that the ones before us who had gone to the right, unlike us, got back home safely. The only information we gleaned from the locals was that we were totally surrounded by the 'Bosch'. We meandered along to the left and everywhere we went kept running into refugees and convoys of Germans. Fortunately we avoided trouble and even the civilians were directing us saying, "Don't go that way – the Bosch are up there".

Still totally oblivious as to where we were and in what direction we were travelling, we eventually decided to pull into a field, conceal the truck as it was now dusk, get our heads down for the night and reconvene the following morning in an attempt to reach the coast. After a fitful night's rest we arose anxious to move on only to discover the truck, together with two of our fellows plus all our kit and personal possessions had gone, leaving us literally with just the clothes we stood up in.

A decision was made to split into small groups and attempt to contact some British. I volunteered to go alone, but my pal, Francis Hill, said he'd come with me, as did a Scots lad called Davy Hewitt. To avoid being seen we moved at night, but as all the road signs had been removed we had no idea in which direction to travel. We wandered around aimlessly for four nights, one of them having walked in a complete circle and frustratingly ending up back where we started. Another night we inadvertently walked into a German convoy. Almost too late we heard voices but fortunately, realising they were not English, were able to beat a hasty retreat. Unbeknown to us this was the big assault on Dunkirk. Looking at a map of the area now tells us we were only about twenty miles distant and had we known we could more than likely have made our way there. However, at the time we had neither maps nor compass and no idea where we were. For all we knew we could well have been in the middle of France. Who knows what would have happened had we been able to make it to Dunkirk. Would we have been lucky enough to board a boat for a safe journey home, or would we have been blown to smithereens on the beach?

Without possessions we had no means of purchasing or bartering for food so were only able to survive by following our natural instincts and stealing eggs (our sole source of sustenance) from various farms, which we swallowed raw. One morning, after a dangerously close encounter with a German convoy during the night, we decided it would be more sensible to travel by day so that at least we could see what was ahead.

Four days later I jumped over a fence, to be confronted by a vehicle coasting down a hill. I jumped back and said to the others "Get under cover, there's a vehicle coming". Not believing me they looked over the fence to see for themselves. In the meantime I was haring up the field, now hotly pursued by the occupants of the vehicle, until eventually Hewitt yelled, "Stop, or they'll kill you". I turned round to see a German Officer and three other soldiers a few yards behind all with Tommy Guns pointing at me. They belonged to a Supply Unit taking ammunition to their troops further up the line.

They were cock-a-hoop at capturing us and it was whilst with them we received our first major scare. When dusk fell our captors pushed us into a field where it was intended we should stay for the night. We were each handed a shovel and told to dig a trench, an instruction that filled us with a sense of foreboding and abject fear. Having heard rumblings about the antics of the Nazis we were convinced we were digging our own graves. Imagine our feeling of relief when it turned out we were actually digging a latrine! Our task completed one German soldier complimented us on the 'nice deep trench' and said we'd made such a good job of it he would give us each some English cigarettes. None of us smoked but we took them as a bartering aid for later on. The Germans possessed loads of 'booty' they'd 'knocked off' as they traversed the line capturing our chaps, and even filled my whisky flask, which had previously contained Cognac, with Johnny Walker Whisky before returning it to me.

The Germans I had anything to do with at this time all seemed well-educated, intelligent people. Most of them could speak English, a lot of them had been to England, knew it as well as their own country, and knew where they were to be sent *when* they got there. I felt sure that if they came to Birmingham and were commanded to set up a Post on the Lickey Hills (just outside the Birmingham border) they would all have known exactly where to go.

Later that evening we travelled on to St. Omer where many allied captives were congregated and over the next few days were moved from place to place in ever increasing numbers. It was night-time when we arrived at St. Omer and were put into a building, which in those days was the Town Hall. We were herded upstairs into a large imposing hall

Town Hall, St. Omer where Gren spent his first night as a POW.

decorated with ornamentation all round, and where the floor was strewn with sleeping captives. In the morning we found we were amongst Dutch, Belgian, French and British captives. I had dossed down next to an elderly British Army Officer, a Lieutenant who was dressed purely in his uniform without any outer covering. The following morning in pouring rain we were marched to a field, and as I had a ground sheet, as well as a sack I had acquired en route, I gave the Lieutenant the sack to put over his shoulders. It seemed that the Germans had confiscated all the bicycles in the area, as there were literally hundreds of them in the field. There were now quite a number of prisoners but the bikes far outnumbered them. Francis grabbed a brand new bike with a three-speed gear so naturally I expected a similar one. However, by this time the Germans had become a bit fed up with me going around being choosy and airing my whims and fancies and in the end one became quite irate and threw me a bike indicating, in an extremely firm tone, "That's yours". I didn't argue! It was a racing type, fixed wheel, no mudguards and dropped handlebars, in fact everything I would not have wished for. Although I'd always had a bike my backside used to get sore very easily so this was the worst sort I could have been issued with.

After we'd cycled a long, long way my chain broke. I dangled it in front of one of the guards to indicate what had happened but he could not have been more disinterested and in a menacing manner gesticulated to me to carry on. The only way I could do so was by scooting the bike along with one foot on a pedal and the other on the floor, which worked perfectly coming downhill but going uphill meant I had to walk. Eventually they took a bike off an elderly Belgian soldier, gave it to me and put him in a cart for the remainder of the journey. That day we cycled until we reached a wool factory, which was packed with fleeces and where we were put for the rest of the day and night without food or water. The following morning broke bright and sunny, and we emerged to find all the bikes had disappeared, presumably having been taken back for use by the next contingent of prisoners. From there on we marched day after day eventually arriving at Cambrai. After the initial day of pouring rain we were fortunate in that the weather was quite good. We quickly became aware of the different types of German soldiers escorting us ranging from the initial well educated ones to those in whose charge we now were who were more on the lines of 'Home Guard' types – older men who bore a grudge against everybody from the First World War and were very reluctant for us to have anything. As we were marched through numerous villages and towns many civilians kindly put buckets of water out for us, but the guards kicked them over rather than let us have a drink. Some people came up with sandwiches or threw a sandwich to us as we marched along, but again the guards snatched them away wherever possible. As we became wise to this Francis patrolled one side of the road, Davy Hewitt the other and I stayed in the middle ready to nip left or right whenever there was the opportunity of acquiring some food and before the guards spotted it. Often it was only a small piece of bread, but to us, who by this time were ravenously hungry, it seemed like manna from heaven. Many more prisoners had joined us and the numbers marching now ran into thousands. I was amazed to see that a preponderance of the French POWs were carrying small suitcases, like attaché cases, as if they were going on holiday. Although guards were alongside pushing us forward I could never understand why the French kept marching. They were in their own country, they could speak the lingo, why were they tolerating being marched along as prisoners? I'm sure, had I been in my own country, I would have thought, "Bugger this, I'm going home, I'll get rid of my uniform and I'm off". Even when we got to the POW Camp they still had their suitcases, but what they contained I never found out.

As we trudged through one little village I became aware of a scuffle on the side nearest to Francis. I dashed over to see what was going on and found we were next to what I presume had been a British Army Stores and Cookhouse. Inside we discovered food, which had been left lying around so I grabbed three or four 7lb tins, having no idea what they contained and not caring; it was food and that was good enough for me. Upon reassembling we compared our 'spoils'. I found I had two tins of beetroot and a tin of potatoes and Francis had a big tin containing about 14lbs of sugar. We felt extremely elated and looked forward to a few good feasts. As we were settling down that night I asked, "Where's that tin of sugar Francis?" He said, "Oh, it was too heavy to carry so I threw it away," which was typical of Francis. Considering this was the first food we'd seen for days and we were all in very real danger of starving, I couldn't believe

31

that having had the good fortune to acquire a tin of sustenance, albeit all sugar, he had then thrown it away because it was too heavy to carry! In civilian life Francis, who was always immaculately manicured, used to wear silver grey slacks and an oatmeal jacket, whereas I sported dark green or grey trousers and dark jacket because I knew very well I would get involved in something. He erred towards clerical work whereas I was a practical chap. If my bike needed a tyre changed I would roll up my sleeves and do it, but Francis would never contemplate doing anything of that sort – he would find someone else to do it for him. Therefore as I didn't mind getting my hands dirty I built up a resistance to germs. Francis, being so meticulously clean, had no resistance whatsoever and, later on, suffered greatly because of this.

Although the guards were pushing us forward they were quite content to march along as, at this stage, they were frequently changed. Presumably they sensed there was no point in our trying to escape, as there was nowhere to escape to and we were safer sticking together and helping each other. On reaching Cambrai we were herded into an old Fort, which was the first place for several days we were offered any food. This was soup, but as the Germans were totally unprepared to cater for such large numbers, it meant most of us queuing for hours as we waited for each individual boiling to take place. From somewhere I'd picked up a little shallow bowl, the only container I possessed in which to hold food. Having eventually acquired my soup, as I came away from the cauldron someone knocked my arm causing me to spill a sufficient amount to considerably reduce my meagre portion. I promptly sat down on the floor and refused to move until I had drunk the remainder.

The following day we were marched to a railway station and herded into closed cattle trucks for transportation to Poland in extreme gloom, the only fraction of light and air coming through slight chinks between the boards of the truck. And so began a nightmare journey lasting four days again without food or water, with fifty people crammed into a truck intended for either eight horses or twenty men. At this stage Paris hadn't fallen and the Germans were still advancing on France so, as the sun blazed down and the heat became ever more intense, we were frequently shunted into sidings to allow German troop trains and hospital trains to pass.

Nevertheless the truck doors remained firmly closed, we were not allowed out for the duration of the journey and natural bodily functions had to be performed in the truck. Due to lack of space most prisoners, except the very weakest, had to stand leaning against each other for support. If one moved all around had to move too. The atmosphere soon became unbearable with the warm weather adding to the heat generated by the men's bodies. In addition to the smell from dirty and sweaty bodies many of the men had dysentery so both the filth and the stench were appalling.

I struck up an acquaintance with one chap, Dennis King, simply because he was standing next to me, seemed to be on his own and I noticed he had a Royal Army Ordnance Corps badge on his cap. He came from Werneth, Oldham, and in civilian life was an instrument mechanic working for Ferranti. He was attached to an Infantry unit, and whereas work was usually sent back to the main Ordnance Corps for repair and maintenance, he had been posted to another unit to do work on site, which explained his isolation. He was very dark skinned and although not a Jew really looked quite Jewish. Later I felt extremely sorry for him as presumably, because of his looks, he was given a very rough time and all the miserable, dirty jobs to do in camp. We became staunch friends, spending a fair amount of time together during the first few months of POW life. After demobilisation he invited me to his wedding in Oldham following which we corresponded for some time, but then letters gradually died out.

Many years after the war, whilst travelling around for the Company for whom I worked, I found myself in Bolton. Realising I was close to Werneth I decided to see if I could look Dennis up. I found his house where there was an elderly lady standing at the gate. I asked her if Dennis King lived there. She said, "He used to but he's been dead for years". I told her how sorry I was and that we had been POWs together. Her face lit up and she said, "Oh, you mean young Dennis". Apparently his father's name was Dennis too. She gave me young Dennis' new address and I went to the house, where his wife still recognised me from all those years ago at their wedding and told me he still worked for Ferranti explaining he did overtime for an hour or two most nights. Just as I was explaining that I could not hang about for too long one of his daughters came in and said she'd take me to the Works to see him. We duly went down to the factory and located the commissionaire who said he would try to get hold of Dennis. That particular day the Firm was holding its Long Service Ceremony and a Mr. Ferranti was presenting the awards. While the commissionaire was attempting to contact Dennis the Ferranti's arrived. Mrs Ferranti was absolutely gorgeous, looking just like a film star. She had a little boy with her who came up to me and started chatting. She came over too and we stood talking together until her husband arrived and off they went. Eventually Dennis arrived spitting fire and brimstone. I'd told his daughter not to say who wanted to see him but to keep my identity secret, and he came out extremely agitated and ranting and raving ready to do battle with whoever it was interrupting such an auspicious occasion. His daughter began to giggle so I waited until the expostulations subsided before stepping forward, when suddenly his gaze fell on me. He mellowed immediately, was absolutely delighted to see me, and all was well. He said, "Next time you are in this area let me know, I'll make sure I've got the evening off, we'll have a meal together and a good old chinwag". We did this on several subsequent occasions but then one time when I called again his wife opened the door with the greeting, "Oh, it's you again". Dennis wasn't there but after such an icy reception, the reason for which I never knew, I beat a hasty retreat and sadly never saw or heard from him again.

Another fellow, Gershwin Ricketts, was also in the same truck as Dennis, Francis and me and seemed, to us nineteen and twenty year olds, an old man. Unfortunately people used to ridicule him as he was bent and had nothing of a military look about him. However, he was quite a character. He was in the Pioneer Corps, which were the army labourers who performed all the menial tasks, and it appeared he'd walked all over England. Later he had a little job in the camp trundling around picking up papers or anything that needed tidying up. Whilst on the train, through a small chink in the wooden boards of the carriage, he spotted the name of a place and said, "We're getting near Luxembourg". The other fellows asked him how the devil he knew that, and not believing a word told him to shut up. But he was right, and months later when we were at Stalag XXB, thinking I would catch him out I said to him, "Do you know Rubery, Gershwin?" "Oh yes", he said, "That's about half way between Birmingham and Bromsgrove". It turned out he knew everywhere from Workhouse to Workhouse.

Back on the journey without any notion of where we were being taken, we were again on the train for four or five days without food or water, eventually arriving at Trier just over the Luxembourg border, by which time everyone was showing signs of wear and tear. We left the train very weak from lack of sustenance, blinking as our eyes smarted from the strong light after the gloom of the enclosed trucks. Struggling to coax our stiff and aching limbs back into working order, we were then marched to a Concentration Camp where we were to spend the night. It was a sunny day and the town was festooned with Nazi flags and banners. The camp was situated at the top of a hill and the route along which we marched was lined with the entire populace of the town – people dressed in Lederhosen who were staunch Hitlerites and who regarded it as great sport to jeer, ridicule, spit upon and boo us as we marched by. What a welcome to the Third Reich! It was very degrading and terribly frightening. I'd never even heard of a Concentration Camp and hadn't a clue what it was. Later on we discovered that the sad inmates already there and dressed in striped pyjamas, were the Jews and Poles who the Germans were systematically sending to the gas chambers.

At last we were fed, albeit extremely frugally, and the following day we re-ran the gauntlet of the local populace and were herded back into our cattle trucks for a further four days' nightmare journey, still having no idea what our destination was to be. By now, together with many of the others, Francis had developed dysentery.

5

THORN – STALAG XXA

Our destination turned out to be Thorn, headquarters of the Prisoner of War Camp Stalag XXA, which was not a single camp, but a multitude of places. According to statistics Stalag XXA contained about 20,000 British prisoners spread over many different Forts or satellite camps. Each camp, which was surrounded by double barbed wire fencing, stood on sandy ground and looked monotonously alike, consisting of row upon row of grey wooden barrack blocks and high wooden watchtowers complete with machine-gun emplacement. Stalag XXA was used as a holding camp for new prisoners who were drafted there pending transportation to other camps. On arrival we were all individually photographed, numbered, given a metal dog tag showing our details (mine says Prisoner of War (Kriegsgefangener), – Camp (Lager), Thorn 7761) which we had to wear round our necks at all times, and we were entered into the filing system, thereby officially becoming an acquisition of the Third Reich. Thus, for the next five years, I totally lost my personal identity officially acquiring the grand title of 'Prisoner of War 7761– Thorn'. The metal dog tags were made so that upon a prisoner's release they could be snapped in half, the Germans keeping one half whilst giving the other to the Prisoner to enable him to be identified when he returned to his own country.

I was housed in Fort 17, which had been a Polish cavalry barracks, basically stables with a small amount of accommodation for the soldiers. The following day various items of our uniform were confiscated and substituted with old Polish clothing. My respectable pair of trousers were taken from me and replaced with a pair of exceedingly tatty and uncomfortable khaki coloured Polish Cavalry trousers. Below the knee these consisted of a piece

Stalag XXA before our uniforms were confiscated. Second from left, Harry Woodhouse, a regular soldier from the Black Country who was killed by friendly fire at the end of the war. Fourth from left, Wilf Jackson.

of loose canvas, which was intended to go inside jackboots. Of course I didn't have jackboots so this just flapped around making my legs extremely cold and causing sores when they got wet. We understood our uniforms had been confiscated to enable German soldiers to be kitted out with British uniforms *when* they invaded Britain, thus allowing them to mingle with the population without drawing attention to themselves.

Our only consolation from being at Stalag XXA was that we now received regular 'food' of sorts. The main meal served at midday was a very wishy washy soup, which varied between barley, barley and potato, and potato and swede, but on rare occasions we had our favourite, a reasonably acceptable type of golden pea. A modicum of meat was added which seemed to be diced pork, but as the soup was cooked in gigantic cauldrons the sprinkling of meat sank to the bottom and appeared virtually non-existent. It was preferable to be at the end of the queue at serving time as by then the watery soup had been dished out and, if you were lucky, the possibility arose of being served with a few slivers of meat. Men were chosen to help clean the potatoes and vegetables but, following a request for cooks to step forward, the soup was then prepared by 'alleged' British Army cooks who were supervised by the Germans. This meant that any Tom, Dick or Harry could claim to have been an official British Army Cook and with hindsight one realises what opportunities were missed. Despite many of the volunteers having no idea how to cook, obviously they were not having the thin soup, and most of the meat found its way into their rations. Although it didn't always materialise, we were supposed to have a piece of ersatz bread each day around teatime. This was a brown bread substitute, exceedingly unpleasant, had both the taste and consistency of having been made from sawdust, and was frequently green with mould on the outside. I estimate a loaf would have been about eight inches long and three and a half to four inches square. This usually had to be shared between five men, sometimes more, but never less than five. Each time we were issued with the bread, to relieve the monotony, five of us grouped together and puzzled about how to share it out. The best way was with a dog tag. The middle piece was removed dog tag width, which would be about one and a half inches. The two remaining pieces were cut lengthwise following which lots were drawn. Five pieces of paper were produced and numbered one to five, then we each drew a number, number one qualifying for first choice. Invariably the middle piece was the best as the loaf sloped away at the ends. By this stage, as we were all feeling the pangs of hunger, and never knew when we would be issued with more bread, a very careful watch was kept to see that the portions were divided completely fairly. That was primarily our daily ration, but there were occasional alternatives. At least once a week we were given biscuits, all different colours, which looked exactly like Spratts dog biscuits. A couple of chaps went off with a blanket to wherever the rations were being distributed; the biscuits were weighed out into the blanket and brought back to be shared between approximately twenty men. We then sat around pondering over them until someone said, "O.K. – how many chaps, we'll start off with ten each shall we?" Each round became less until we usually ended by breaking a biscuit in half to enable every man to have an equal portion. Another issue was knäckebrot, a Ryvita type crispbread, which came in packets and was easy to distribute. I have no recollection of having any spread such as margarine but on rare occasions we did get a smattering of jam. In the morning we had a drink made from acorns, no sweetener, no milk, it was just a brown, bitter sludge, which the Germans called coffee. An alternative to that was a mint tea, which was equally delicious!! Occasionally we had white, soft cheese, rather like cottage cheese, but considerably less pleasant. Later, when we were slightly better fed, some chaps worked in the factory making that particular cheese. When it was time to draw the rations the Germans couldn't understand why the cheese was thrown on the floor. We'd been pre-warned what our comrades had done to it before it left the factory and, hungry as we were, had no intention of consuming it.

We were now issued with a blanket each and a mess tin provided from a variety of mess tins of different nationalities, which had been confiscated by the Germans. Prior to that some chaps had only possessed a tin can in which to put their soup. We were also given a small slab of soap which gave no lather whatsoever, was more like a pumice stone and rubbed your skin off, and what was alleged to be a towel, a coarse, very hard huckaback type towel, which simply pushed the water around and was useless for drying. We were issued with clogs, typical Dutch sabots that were very uncomfortable. It was compulsory to wear them to save our boots but if we had to run, as we frequently did when hustled along on parade, there was a tendency for the sabot to slide forward and the bridge of the foot to catch on the back edge, which was extremely painful. In addition, and more pleasant to wear, were the issue of what they called pantoffels, a wooden base with a piece of material over the top and without a back – rather like mules.

During the war many work camps were set up in Poland to house soldiers and airmen. Under the Geneva Convention those below the rank of Sergeant were obliged to work, but Officers and senior NCOs, who were excused this obligation, were housed in separate camps. Large camps such as Stalag XXA at Thorn or Stalag XXB at Marienburg had a main compound and as many as five hundred satellite work camps, usually in the surrounding area but sometimes up to a distance of two hundred miles away. Some were just a bunkhouse at a farm, others a quarry holding a dozen prisoners plus a few guards. The ordinary ranks, of whom there were many thousands, worked on the land, in mines, in factories or anywhere that did not involve directly helping the enemy's war effort. Most prisoners were grudgingly agreeable to this as at least it relieved the boredom and intense monotony of camp life and gave them the opportunity to scrounge extra food once outside the barbed wire fence.

Nobody seemed to know which British Officer should be in charge of the prisoners in the camp but the Officer who somehow became appointed whilst we were in Stalag XXA was a tall, smart Company Sergeant Major by the name of Homer, a regular soldier from the Rifle Brigade. Assuming that the Germans were going to win the war, he gave the impression from the word go that *he* wanted to be on the winning side. He was always very smartly dressed with his trousers pressed, kept his uniform intact, and did not have any items of clothing taken from him. I don't think he actually lived inside the camp, but was just the other side of the wire, and was quite happy to hand out orders from the Germans. He had a 'toady', a Lance Corporal who followed him around carrying a little stool. Every time Homer, who was over six feet tall, stopped the stool was put down for him to stand on. I did see him again on the march at the end of the war and happened to mention to some others that I knew him when he was at Fort 17, adding "He was a right so and so". They said, "Oh, he's quite a decent chap". It appeared that, with the fortunes of war changing, he'd reverted to the winning side again. He was not very 'British', and not a likeable man at all.

One job I was deputed to perform whilst at Thorn was logging in a forest. We were marched to the forest where trees had been felled, cut into lengths, and we spent two or three days moving the logs around and stacking them. As far as we knew there was no purpose to this occupation other than to find us some heavy labour. The Germans were determined to find us something to do and we needed a darned good reason to be excused working. I think we were paid for that job, not with Deutschmarks but with Largergelt, money that was printed specifically for POWs. It had no value whatsoever as there was nothing to spend it on, but later on in other camps we did have a little canteen, despite the fact that commodities in it were virtually non-existent. The chaps primarily used the Largergelt for bets when playing cards, and some of them became millionaires with this worthless money! We only received a pittance, a matter of pence, for a whole day's work, although when doing regular work, such as on a farm or in a factory the pay was slightly greater, but still not a lot.

Another day we were sent to a German Barracks to do chores. We were actually sent inside the barracks where I was amazed to find the amount of information displayed relevant to the British. The walls were plastered with designs of weaponry, aircraft, ships, tanks, uniforms, badges of rank, etc. etc. – they were really well organised and seemed to know everything about us whereas we didn't even know who they were. All I'd seen about the Germans was in the picture houses, pictures of Nazis displaying German swastikas as they marched. I was extremely surprised to learn that they were all obliged to attend choir classes. Whereas we sometimes sang any old song that came into our minds, such as *It's a Long Way to Tipperary*, to help keep spirits up and help us keep in step as we marched along, each German service had its own specific official military marching song, sung in harmony, and which, I have to admit, sounded most impressive. During rehearsal we joined in putting our own interpretation on the words relevant to the privations of the conditions in camp and the food!

A conduit, in which rough holes had been bored at intervals, provided the meagre, extremely inadequate, washing facilities in the camp and between certain times each day cold water dribbled through to allow us to wash as best we could. We lived in the same clothes that had originally been issued to us when our uniforms were confiscated, but as no hot water was provided washing them was totally out of the question. Consequently because of the insanitary conditions and sleeping rough on straw everyone soon became infested with lice, which was then conducive to the development of Scabies. Having now developed this unpleasant infestation, I was sent to Fort 14, which was set up as a hospital housing many prisoners with serious illnesses. Facilities there were marginally better with individual beds and showers. To treat the Scabies buckets of dark brown ointment, resembling the consistency of mud, were provided. This had to be plastered all over the body ensuring it was well rubbed into all the hairy parts. Following this treatment we were given a white paste to rub on our skin prior to the shower being turned on, which resulted in a very uncomfortable experience as upon contact with water the ointment burned like fury.

During my spell in hospital the name Gandy kept cropping up and eventually I met this fellow who came from Darlaston. He was a hard man, very swarthy, wore army issue steel framed spectacles, and all his hair had been shaved off. I became friendly with him and for the remainder of my POW days kept bumping into him. He was a Bombardier in the Royal Artillery, was very well educated, had a typical Black Country accent and told me his full name was Ivanhoe Austin Gandy, commonly known as Ivan.

Because Scabies had now become so rife it was decreed that everybody's head was to be shaved. We had two or three camp barbers who delighted in having somebody in the chair just before roll-call, which took place each morning and evening. To our great amusement the unfortunate victim in the chair when roll-call came could arrive with half his head shaved, a swastika cut in his hair or a variety of various other shapes and designs. Following roll-call he then had to return to be finished off to an acceptable standard. Before I left the hospital I persuaded Ivan to give me a crew cut, which, for some unknown reason, I was allowed to get away with, never having my head completely shaved.

One day some Red Cross parcels arrived containing limited articles of clothing. A lottery was devised with the name of each article being itemised on individual pieces of paper which were then put, together with innumerable blanks, into a pile, and everyone selected a piece. When my turn came I was duly issued with a pair of pink striped pyjamas. Nothing daunted I used the jacket as a shirt, initially I wore the trousers underneath my cavalry trousers to give added warmth, and later on, when I was in Stalag XXB I cut the legs off and made them into a pair of shorts. Together with a bit of ingenuity these proved to be a very useful acquisition.

The Germans, being signatories to the Geneva Convention, were expected to honour the rules laid down therein, which stated that it was the duty of the military authorities of the holding country of prisoners to adequately feed and clothe them. The rations of prisoners were supposed to equal those allocated to a private soldier of the 'host' country; therefore, it was assumed by the authorities back home that Red Cross parcels simply provided extras. How extremely incorrect this thinking turned out to be as we soon became dependant upon the Red Cross and family parcels that *did* manage to reach us, for our basic survival. When Red Cross food parcels eventually came through, the commandant, a most peculiar fellow, decided to restrict allocation, advocating that if he issued a parcel to each person they would immediately devour all the contents and make themselves ill. Presumably he didn't fancy having a couple of hundred chaps on sick parade! I suppose it could have been logical, but only allowing one parcel between six fellows made it very difficult to distribute the contents as each parcel contained a variety of individual items. By this time the possibility of starvation was becoming very real, so to share items round as fairly as possible we put them into equal piles and drew lots. This didn't please some of the chaps who, by now having abandoned a spirit of sharing, would grab all they could get. Day and night we were all in a perpetual state of hunger and to some, half crazed by the agonisingly gnawing pangs, complete selfishness set in. Arguments and fights broke out, a state of 'dog eat dog' arose and 'grab all you can get' from the meagre rations on offer. At first all the Red Cross parcels were British and each one contained a meat loaf made by a firm called Lustys. This was in a fair sized tin, therefore taking up a lot of room, but turned out to be completely inedible. When the tin was punctured the stench was obnoxious and they all had to be thrown away. By using extremely inferior meat Lustys must have made a fortune out of POWs.

Escape from the camp was a virtual impossibility. I only heard of one escapee who managed to get safely back home. Occasionally tins of Colman's Mustard arrived in camp in the British Red Cross parcels and beneath the part of the label that was glued to the tin his number had been written. This was the sign of a successful escape.

Every day a group of chaps from Fort 17 went to an Offlag (an Officers' camp) to perform chores such as peel potatoes, tidy up etc. Came the day when, after a great deal of planning, four Airforce Officers from the Offlag swapped uniforms and identities with four of our army privates, and returned to camp that night with our party. Another group of chaps who worked at the local aerodrome managed to commandeer some overalls belonging to German Airforce mechanics. The following morning three of the officers went to the aerodrome with our working party with the intention of stealing a plane to fly home, and the fourth swapped identity with a chap who was detailed to join a working party at a farm. This meant one going in one direction and the other three the opposite way. Upon reaching the aerodrome the three dressed themselves in the mechanics' overalls and headed towards a plane, unfortunately not realising that particular area was out of bounds to mechanics. Officials soon descended upon them and began asking questions. Being unable to speak German their plan was rumbled, their identities soon became apparent and they were escorted back to their Offlag whereupon their entire camp was ordered out on parade. The Guards informed the internees that the Airforce Officers had been captured, and suggested that, to save a lot of 'hastle', it would be better for all if the people with whom they had swapped would step forward. After some reluctance, and to avoid further repercussions, the four chaps stepped forward, which caused great consternation as the Germans had only captured three, so where was the fourth? Interest now switched to Fort 17 where we were all put on parade and the very lengthy process of identification took place. Photographs were brought from HQ and we all had to be individually identified by comparing us with the photographs and our dog tag numbers. This took several hours during which time we were made to stand on parade. It was eventually discovered that the fourth chap had gone to the farm, but we heard nothing more about him and from stories circulating later understood he never arrived so, as far as we all knew, got away. That was quite an exciting event, which livened up our exceedingly humdrum lives for a short while.

As is the wont of 'squaddies' we formed a concert party and a hut was designated for the periodic performance of concerts. We were amazed at the talent some of the chaps possessed and some excellent performances took place. I remember one fellow, Tommy Power, whose voice matched his name; he possessed a really powerful singing voice. We formed a small orchestra with an accordion player, a clarinetist, and several mouth organs, an instrument that was very popular at the time, some being true harmonica players with a slide to change key. I took part in concerts later on but not at this particular period.

When a new intake arrived at the camp everyone flocked to the gates to see if there was anybody they recognised. On one occasion a chap arrived who looked familiar to me; I thought he had been an apprentice at the

Austin. His name was Neville Jones and he later explained the resemblance to me by saying he wasn't the chap I knew but was his cousin. Neville told me he worked at the Austin as a test pilot for the Fairey Battle, the first of which aircraft was flown out of the Works in 1937 from the flying ground on site. I could only recall one test pilot there named Neville Stack. It struck me as being somewhat queer. If this chap was a test pilot why was he here in army uniform – why hadn't he joined the airforce? Anyway I was in no position to argue. I saw him periodically and we chatted together; then, the night before I was due to leave the camp to go to Langfur, I told him I was off the following morning with a working party and wished I had some bread. He asked if I had any genuine German money. I don't remember how I had acquired them but I had a few German marks. He said if I would give them to him he would get me a loaf of bread. Delighted I gave him the money – and never saw him again! The following morning, in very dejected mood, I set off, minus my few marks and without any bread, vowing that if ever I saw Neville Jones again he would be in deep trouble. When I did meet him again some years later in Stalag XXB he'd forgotten he was a test pilot and was now admitting to being an apprentice at the Austin. Equally by this time I'd mellowed and had no wish for retribution so just ignored him.

Following the war, when I returned to my job at the Austin and came to live in my present house, I discovered his stepmother lived two doors away. It turned out my mate Tom was leaving his job in the toolroom office at the Austin and Neville had been appointed to take his place. When he knew who his replacement was Tom asked me to meet him saying, "He's got a lot in common with you, he was a POW", but upon discovering who it was I declined the invitation not wishing to have anything at all to do with him.

Francis was soon sent to work on a farm and eventually I was sent with a party of approximately one hundred to work at Langfur which was some distance away from our present camp and necessitated yet another train journey. Whilst there we were accommodated in a camp, set up on the farm in a barn which had two floors, and where bunk beds, tables and benches had been provided for our use all in the same room. It had been well cleaned and, to our surprise, really was quite acceptable. Two Company Sergeant Majors from the Queen Victoria Rifles were in charge and they, together with the cook, who was also from the same Regiment, bunked downstairs. Bert Deacon and Ray Allbrow were also there, so as I had made acquaintance with Bert earlier at Fort 17, we palled up together and were on the upper floor.

The farm, which would originally have been Polish before the German occupation, was not arable, although there were a lot of fruit trees growing around it, but was more like a smallholding. We were sent there to transfer soil from this area to a local airfield which was being extended and which, incidentally is now a very large Commercial Airport. A few days after arriving a German Unteroffizer (equivalent of a Sergeant in the British Army), who spoke excellent English, approached me and asked what the food was like. I replied, "Not very good" and described what we had. The following day, after the Unteroffizer had checked the rations, he told me we were receiving what we were supposed to be having and (as I understood it – not being very good at German) it was going to get worse. With a sinking heart I told the other chaps who all groaned. However, following his visit, and much to our surprise and delight, we began occasionally to be served sausage as it turned out he had actually said we were going to get Wurst.

Prior to my return visit in 2000 I visited the Polish parents of a friend of my youngest daughter Kim. I mentioned Wrzeszcz (Langfur) (the names have now all been changed) and the man told me that when he flies back to Poland he always flies to that airport.

The owner of the farm, a big man, was a Sergeant Major in the airforce. Our job was to dig soil out of a field and load it into trucks on a type of mini railway system, which then transported it to the airfield. The train took the full trucks away, brought back empties and parked them along the siding so that we could work continuously. We began by digging out one rut down the side of the field. The chaps digging out the soil threw it onto the bank and the chap on the bank threw it into the truck. As the rut got bigger another rut was begun down the other side. If we dug *down* too far it made the work extremely heavy so we kept digging out sideways.

A German civilian, who was in charge of the project, walked up and down supervising while the two Sergeant Majors from our billet also patrolled, one either side. At first I couldn't understand what they were supposed to be doing, but I found out one day! When the civilian boss

Gren front left, behind him Bert Deacon and on extreme right Ray Allbrow digging out soil to make an airfield in Poland. Photo taken by one of the guards, and sent to Gren by Ray, together with the following letter, in December 1988.

'Hi Gren,

   Surprise surprise, remember this photo and can you remember what was making us look as though we were enjoying ourselves? Well when Fritz (on the right) had set the camera up he trotted by me and you said, "You should have tripped him up". I'd hate to think what would have happened if I had, but it seemed funny at the time. This was at Langfur. I bet it will bring back a few memories. It was three years later at Kielau when I saw the photo. Fritz joined our working party – he had been promoted. (He was a right B.............!) Some time later he got orders that the Russian Front awaited, so he got well and truly drunk. I went to his office and told a few lies like what a good chap he was, and we were sad to see him go. This did the trick, he got his photo album out and we started having a look. Of course there were quite a few girl friends then lo and behold there it was, the photo that I had forgotten. I asked him for it 'Nien!' I said he could take another off, and in any case I would like to have his photo so he tore it out and gave it to me and that's the end of that little story.

   Well cheerio for now Gren.

   Have a really good Christmas and all the very best wishes for the New Year
   Ray'

came along and found a truck fully loaded, he instructed us to push it to the other trucks and link them all together ready to be pulled away. Came the day when our truck was fully loaded and he was nowhere to be seen so one of our Sergeant Majors decided to assume authority and ordered us to push the trucks together. I was the first one on the line to whom he said, "Go on – push the trucks up". I said, "Pardon". He said, "Push the trucks up they'll be coming for them". I said, "So what, when the supervisor comes we can push them together, but not before". At that point he and I entered into a heated debate, as I demanded to know which side of the war effort he was on – was he one of us, or was he one of them? He became quite irate, and I wasn't particularly calm either! He said, "I'll report you to the Commandant" to which I replied, "Good on yer mate". When we got back to camp that evening before dismissing us I saw him go to the Commandant and chat to him. The Commandant called me over and through the interpreter he was told that I had refused to obey the Sergeant Major. Upon admitting I had I was informed that I would not go to the airfield with the workers the next day, but would stay in the camp. The following morning when the others went off to work, another chap called Jeffries (who advocated he was a professional footballer either with Queens Park Rangers or Crystal Palace) who also had fallen foul of the authorities, and I were jointly put on 'Jankers'. We were told that there was a cesspit in the compound and we were to empty it. I must admit it was quite obnoxious initially but became lovable later on. We were given a wooden box with handles either side, and a large ladle. We ladled the contents out of the cesspit into the box and then took it through the guards' quarters, down to the orchard and dumped the contents around the fruit trees. Nothing could have been more acceptable. We thought of all the others slogging their guts out digging a hole in the ground while Jeffries and I were on our own with nobody at all to bother us. We took our box down to the orchard, had a sit down, picked sufficient apples both to eat there and to take back to the billet – and, of course, made this as long-winded a process as was possible. At lunchtime the guards' food arrived in milk churns, which we then had to clean out. Invariably there was food left in them, much better than we had, so we helped ourselves. The commandant's wife was very compassionate towards us and at lunchtime, when the guards were having their meal, gave us a packet of sandwiches (which we couldn't eat slowly enough) and at night time a packet of cigarettes. When we did ultimately succeed in emptying the cesspit we saw some boards, went to investigate, and to our delight found another one, which the authorities knew nothing about. As naturally we wanted to be very thorough in our punishment, we proceeded to empty this cesspit too, which enabled us to make the job last for several weeks.

Another part of my 'Jankers' was to sweep our room in the camp. In the evening the boys would sit around playing cards or reading. As the room couldn't be swept until everyone was in bed, I soon turned this to my advantage, and beat all the others to bed, consequently when the guard arrived, asked for Davies and was informed that I was in bed, he delegated someone else to do the job. This was the best bit of punishment I'd ever had!

I don't know whether the Germans eventually realised we were conning them by digging out sideways at the airfield, but they decided to import some Italian POWs to take over from us. Initially a hundred were expected which necessitated the construction of a building in which to accommodate them. I was instructed to assist the civilian builders erecting this and was put to work mixing cement for a bricklayer, which was another cushy little number as I was spared the long march down the road to the hole. Some of the work looked a little suspect as again, when the request went out for qualified bricklayers, a few questionable ones, who fancied having a go, claimed to be skilled at the job.

Around September time, the rations remained constant, but I was able to supplement mine with a few extra bits and pieces remaining from my punishment. My twenty-first birthday was imminent and, as a celebration, I was determined I was going to have a bit of bread instead of the revolting issue of 'dog' biscuits. To make this possible I saved a small piece from our meagre bread allocation, but, being somewhat less than fresh by the date of my birthday, this was not very palatable. A Welsh chap, who slept in the bunk above me and was a bit of a loner, had somehow managed to acquire a loaf of white bread (probably flogged something to a civilian). He very kindly gave me the knob end of his loaf as my birthday present.

Another Welshman who was there, a guardsman, who had hair clippers and scissors, agreed to cut the chaps' hair in exchange for a cigarette. He seemed to have a permanent queue so as I fancied having a go at hair cutting I went to see him and suggested I gave him a hand. He asked if I could cut hair to which I replied, "Not really, but if I run the clippers up the chaps' heads you could finish them off with the scissors". I told him I didn't want anything for it but would just like to have a go. He agreed and I called in the next chap. Suddenly there was a distinct absence of people queuing, but my mate Bert Deacon decided that as he wasn't going anywhere for a day or two I could practise on him! After a short while I became so proficient that the men began to ask for *my* services, and later on, when I was sent away to work on a farm, I was delegated the job of camp barber.

Many years later, as I was walking along the front at St. Leonard's outside Hastings, where I had been sent to convalesce, I espied a Travel Agency Board advertising trips to various places one of which was Biddenden. This rang a bell and I felt sure it was where Bert came from. I enquired whether it was associated with Siamese Twins, and upon being told, "Oh yes, The Maids of Biddenden", I decided to visit the following day. Bert, an extremely nice and handsome chap who worked in the grocer's shop, had married his girlfriend Mildred just before coming to France. He was in the same truck as me going to Thorn and initially we were billeted in the same room. When our first mail came through his letter was from Mildred saying that she'd lost their baby. Sadly they never had another child. He was also a bell ringer and did a lot of work for his local church. He had always described Biddenden as a little country village, but by the time I visited it had grown into a fairly large town with many modern houses, and had become a commuter base for people travelling to London. My heart sank as I presumed there would be little possibility of finding Bert now but I went into the Post Office and asked the gentleman if he happened to know Bert Deacon. Although only having been there for a year or two, because Bert was a bell ringer, he did know him. He told me where he lived and I went round to his house. No reply, so I went to the house next door where the woman said, "If you want to know anything about *him* you'll have to go and see that woman over there". I went 'over there' to be met by a Welsh lady, very friendly, very amicable who told me Bert was at work at British Gates and his wife worked there part-time too.

Eventually I found British Gates, went into the office in the yard and asked the chap if he knew Bert Deacon. He said, "That's his desk over there but he's in the yard with a customer at the moment", so I asked him if he would mind fetching Bert for me. It was a scorching hot day and I was in shirt sleeves and wearing sunglasses. Obviously we had both changed considerably since our army days and he didn't recognise me when he

An illicit photo taken in Stalag XXA. When I came back from the farm the accommodation had been extended and these new barracks had been built. On the left is me and on the right is Benny Higgs who was in my Unit. It was through his influence that I was later delegated the job of heaving coal on the railway. Before the war Benny worked at the Austin as an apprentice carpenter but when we returned there after hostilities he was appointed Inspector on the Production Track. He disliked that job so emigrated to Canada. One day Mair (my wife) and I were returning from a trip into Birmingham when she said she fancied an ice cream. I stopped in Selly Oak (a short distance from where we lived) and entered a shop to find, to my amazement, the proprietor was Benny Higgs who, unbeknown to me, had returned to this country.

came into the office with a cheery "Good morning Sir, can I help you?" Jocularly, and fully unaware of his job description, I said, "Oh yes, I'm from Customs and Excise and we've had a lot of complaints about the products you are turning out at this factory". Bert, a British Gates man through and through, was hit personally by this remark. I elaborated a little about the complaints and he began visibly to tremble with fury. I inserted a little German phrase into the conversation hoping to give him a clue, but he was too furious to notice. He went to sit behind his desk and lit up his pipe in order to regain his composure, at which point I took off my sunglasses. He looked at me again and burst out "Grenville, you bugger". He fetched his wife, introduced her to me and we agreed to meet at his home the next day when we had a great time together. We enjoyed each other's company so much that later my wife and I spent a holiday with them at their home. The following year Bert and his wife were due to visit Birmingham to stay with us, but before they could do so his wife, a farm girl who looked as strong as an ox, was diagnosed with Cancer and very sadly died shortly afterwards. Bert continued to visit, and stay with me, at intervals following his wife's death until it became too much for him, but we still correspond once a year at Christmas.

The last job I remember doing at Langfur was finishing off a chimney. I was on the roof with the cement in part of a cask. After completing the job I began to descend the ladder but had difficulty in manipulating the cask off the roof so in the end decided to drop it, hoping and praying it would drop on its face – it didn't. I ended up with two metal rings, a lot of pieces of wood, and left over cement strewn around a large area, which did not please the guard one little bit!

6

STALAG XXB – MARIENBURG – THE CAMP

Not long after this incident occurred we were moved from Stalag XXA to Stalag XXB. British and American prisoners were spread over the whole of Germany in many different camps, but the majority were placed furthest to the east in the Stalags, as far away from home as possible in order to deter escapes. The headquarters of Stalag XXB was actually at Willenberg, which was a suburb on the outskirts of the town of Marienburg. It was a very large camp containing French, Belgians and later Serbs, but was primarily for British prisoners. According to War Office figures published on 1st December 1944 there were 25,000 prisoners distributed throughout the Marienburg main and satellite camps, 9,173 of them being British and Commonwealth prisoners, 856 of whom were in the main camp. (Lack of precise details makes it difficult to obtain official information but it was estimated that in the middle of 1944 Germany had captured nine million Prisoners of War of various nationalities. However, this is misleading as it omits to take into account millions of captured Russian soldiers in the east who, through neglect and lack of food, had already perished). The town was down below the camp, which was on a plateau on top of a hill beside the river Nogat the camp overlooking the river on one side. Upon entering through the main gates, part of a room on the right was specified as a library, although it only contained a handful of books. It was not a library in the sense that we know the word but was somewhere where chaps could play cards, the main games played being solo whist and cribbage, which Bert taught me how to play. There was also a small shop. The only thing I remember buying from there was mustard, which we spread on our bread to give it a bit of flavour. Junak cigarettes, which were Polish, were also sold there. These were quite long but very thin, half of them being hollow cardboard (like a filter tip) and the other half paper filled with sweepings off the floor, which resembled tobacco. Unless chaps, who bought them with their Largergelt, were extremely careful the 'tobacco', which was very loosely packed, would drop out before the cigarette was lit. The sickbay was in the same block and beyond it were the French and Belgian quarters. The guards were housed in a compound outside the main gate. Down both sides running the length of the camp, and along the bottom, were the wooden huts. The far end was vacant when we arrived but eventually became fenced off and housed a small group of Serbs, possibly around 100. This still left the Brits as the predominant group, there being about 100 of us in each hut. The bunks, which ran the length of the room, were three tiers high, the bottom tier being approximately six inches off the ground, and were just like trays

Gren, back row left, with a group of Welsh soldiers. When official photographs of POWs in Stalag XXB were taken I decided, (as a Welshman) that I would prefer to be included in the Welsh, rather than the British, group.

consisting of wooden slats on which was a palliasse. Everybody tried to get the top bunk as the rubbish from that person fell on to the middle, then down to the bottom chap who caught the lot. As in Stalag XXA boards divided each person's patch, again allowing a width of approximately two and a half feet per person, with a board, approximately three inches high, giving the only privacy from the adjacent patch.

Beyond the huts was the river Nogat and then into no-man's land. A single strand of barbed wire hung two or three feet from the ground on which the Germans strung black painted skulls in order to strike terror into the hearts of every prisoner. Anyone venturing beyond the barbed wire was liable to be shot. Approximately six feet beyond the single strand of wire there were eight foot fences set four feet apart, with rolls of barbed wire between the two. High watchtowers were placed in each corner mounted with machine guns, and guards with dogs permanently patrolled the perimeter.

The winters were extremely severe, temperatures staying at 20° below zero for months at a time. The amount of fuel allocated to feed the one small iron stove in each hut was negligible, therefore in a vain attempt to keep warm, we systematically stripped, and fed into the stove, a slatted board from the base of each bunk, until we were in grave danger of falling through. Down the centre of the hut was a wooden table with benches. Up the river side, which housed the French and Belgians, were the latrines and washhouse. The latrine was just a pit draining down into the river with crossed poles at either end holding a pole across the middle on which you perched as best you could, bodily functions being performed without the provision of such luxuries as toilet paper. The washing facility was again a conduit with holes banged into it, out of which trickled the minimum amount of icy cold water. There was also a standpipe under which I used to crouch so that I could quickly immerse myself and get it all over in one go instead of waiting for the trickle from the conduit. The cookhouse was on the left of the gate. The prisoners did the cooking again with Germans in charge. Behind the cookhouse was the Bunker (the cell block), which could accommodate about a dozen individual prisoners in solitary confinement; a brick built construction fenced off from the rest of the camp, though prisoners could converse with others through the fence when they were brought out for parade. On a higher level above that was what was known as the Straffelager, which was just like an ordinary barrack room, where people who were pending conviction for having committed some crime or other, were held awaiting sentence.

The camp, situated on the sandy Baltic coastal plain, was rife with fleas. The fleas did battle with the lice, the lice materialising through the lack of adequate hygiene facilities. It was impossible, in such atrocious conditions, to avoid becoming infested with both. It was a very large camp with a high-ranking German Officer in charge. During my time there we had a variety of Commandants, some being extremely nasty people, but others

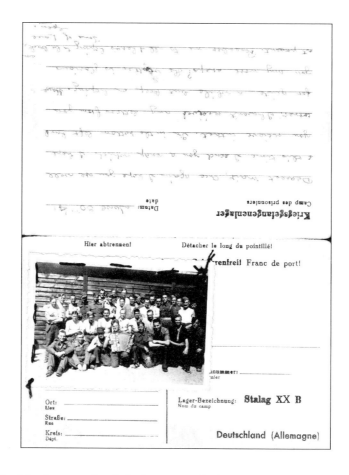

Letter card with photograph stitched onto it which Gren sent to his girlfriend Mair who later became his wife.

reasonably acceptable. I remember one fellow in particular who, prior to France being invaded, had been captured in that country by the Durham Light Infantry. Apparently they had given him a rough time so, when he became Camp Commandant, he went round looking for prisoners with a DLI badge in order to gain retribution – a very unpleasant person indeed. Any new intakes arriving from the Durham Light Infantry were immediately advised to remove their badge.

Prisoners were allowed four PC's and two three-sided Letter Cards a month to write home. Not everyone had homes or wanted to write home so with cigarettes we were able to barter for further supplies. Obviously these were all thoroughly vetted before being sent and did not allow much room for news so the writing had to be severely condensed. Before my posting to France, despite the fact we were not supposed to, I told father I would do my best to keep him informed of my whereabouts. We agreed that at each place I visited which I thought would be on a map, I would address his correspondence with two letters portraying the name of the place, i.e. when we were at Carvin, I first put Mr C.A. Davies. Next I addressed it to Mr R.V. Davies and the next Mr I.N. Davies. He could then piece these letters together to know where I was. One of the first places I was stationed at was Bethune. That was easy – Mr. B.E. Davies, then Mr T.H. Davies, (which were my father's initials anyway) but as soon as he received the B.E. he replied telling me he knew I was in Bethune. This was at a time when mail came through uncensored and before I was taken Prisoner. When I was interned at Thorn I was back to Mr T.H. Davies again, which made it a bit confusing, and I also feared with the censoring, the authorities might cotton on to what I was doing, but fortunately relatives had been informed by the Red Cross when we were taken prisoner telling them where camps were. This was just as well for when I was at Willenberg, and only able to send one card a month, I feared the war would be over before I could send the full name to my father!

In the British Section we had a doctor and a Roman Catholic priest, who was a regular soldier with one of the Scottish regiments, both of whom were army officers, and Captain King who was the Church of England priest. He came from Newton Abbott and was a bit of a 'toff'. After the war, my landlady in Rubery had a sister living in Newton Abbott who came visiting when I was there. Mention was made of Captain King and I was told he'd got into financial difficulties and by volunteering to serve in the army as a priest had managed to wipe out all his debts. However, he was an awfully nice person and a perfect gentleman.

Officially the British section of the camp should have been run by a Senior Ranking British internee but, although we did have one or two Regimental Sergeant Majors, Willenberg was run by a chap called Charlie McDowell. It was said that Charlie was a Corporal in the Gordon Highlanders, a regular soldier, an Indian Army boxing champ, was amongst the first group to be moved into the camp in its infancy and had assumed control right from the beginning. He was in charge, he maintained his authority throughout and nobody ever dared overrule him. Later we acquired RSMs and CSMs by the bucket load but Charlie always remained in charge even though he never wore a badge of rank – his uniform was totally undecorated. He was a bullyboy and always had his little group of henchmen along with him. I struck up a friendship with Gordon Downie, a Glaswegian Customs and Excise Officer who, sometime after the war finished, was transferred to work in the Distilleries in Aberdeen. One day he wrote to me saying he'd met Charlie McDowell working as a postman in Glasgow. It seemed extraordinary that in each camp someone tended to take control who was anxious to join the winning side. Charlie was very reminiscent of Homer in Stalag XXA who always strutted about like a peacock. A strong rumour also circulated that in another Fort in Thorn the British chap in charge went around giving the orders for the Germans in a very menacing way, and was actually issued with a revolver to enable him to do so.

In between me being sent out on one job and returning a large pool had been dug in the compound. The chaps hoped it was going to be a swimming pool but it transpired it was to be used in the event of fire. Obviously with all huts made of wood fire was a very real hazard. The camp itself was basically a working camp, not a Colditz type where the internees had nothing to do. Some prisoners were sent out daily to work in the locality and others were sent longer distances, too far to return each night, where an interim camp would be set up on site. The first job I was sent to took me away for a year.

At one point I developed an ulcerated leg, which was very unpleasant and painful, and, because of lack of nourishment, refused to heal, therefore I was excused duties for the time being. Having no wish to aid the German cause, by swinging the lead a little I managed to avoid work for a year. As soon as my leg began to heal I would 'inadvertently' bump it and break it open again enabling me to spend much of that particular year in sickbay, which was a lot cleaner than the camp itself, and alleviated a lot of problems. Unfortunately the beds were no more comfortable being exactly the same as in the huts. There were at least two roll calls a day but hospitalised cases were excused parade being counted in their bunks. Corporal Thompson from the Medical Corps who looked after the sickbay and was a first class medical chap, eventually worked out how to heal the ulcers suffered by many of the men. He surrounded the wound with Vaseline, crushed M&B tablets sent from Britain, and put the resulting powder on top of the wound. This was then bandaged and left to do its work for two weeks, at which point

Group of British POWs in Stalag XXB with one of the accordianists who took part in concert parties. Gren third from right front row (sporting collar and tie).

each patient breathed a huge sigh of relief knowing he was excused duties for another fortnight. Whilst I was in sickbay we organised a concert party in which I participated in a singing group. Thompson was obviously responsible for getting the occupants well enough to return to duties, but being interested in music, he started a choir. Having a reasonable voice I joined, and have a sneaking suspicion he kept me in hospital a bit longer to boost his choir. During the concerts the Germans were always in attendance sitting at the front to keep an eye on everyone.

One day a young chap was brought to the hospital, and as I'd been in there for such a long time Thompson brought the lad to me on the day of the concert asking me to keep my eye on him as he was afraid he was going 'round the bend'. Whilst chatting to the lad I became aware he had a blade in one hand with which he kept making little cuts on his arm, seemingly in an attempt to cut an artery, but almost as though this was only pretence.

POWs in Stalag XXB wrapped up against the forthcoming bitter winter weather and all wearing the same uniform coats, which had arrived in Red Cross parcels. Third from right back row, Ivanhoe Austin Gandy who kept escaping.

After a few minutes I suggested he put the blade away at which point he informed me that he'd got to kill himself. I asked why and in great confidence he told me he had a dead baby inside him. I managed to persuade him to come to the concert that night and afterwards he insisted he'd enjoyed it. However, during the course of the night he vanished and was found next morning drowned in the pond that had been dug in case of fire. A classic example of how low a chap's morale could get and in actual fact we had several people commit suicide, invariably in the toilets where they would hang themselves.

In an attempt to keep spirits up, and as the boys became slightly more robust, we organised international football matches – Scotland and Wales against England and Ireland. At one point we also organised a small athletic meeting, which proved to be very heavy going as the parade area consisted totally of sandy ground.

I believe it was an agreement with this country to keep us supplied with as much uniform as possible, and occasionally dribs and drabs filtered through from the homeland in the Red Cross parcels. In a big camp like Stalag XXB we were supposed to have one parcel a week but it didn't work out like that. There were two types of Red Cross parcels, British, and Canadian which were far superior to the British. We never knew which we were going to receive, or, indeed, if we would receive one at all, as the food was regarded as surplus to our requirements. Although some prisoners never received anything, at times parcels were received from home. I was lucky as my father and one or two of our neighbours occasionally clubbed together to send me chocolates. Father also sent me a pair of boots, which meant that for a long time I had the luxury of two pairs. The authorities supplied us with Czechoslovakian boots on one occasion which were all the same size. They were rather like natural leather, very much like cardboard, light brown in colour and extremely uncomfortable.

Some charitable organisations, which were set up in Britain, had lists of people whose sons were POWs. One day I received a small parcel (I have an idea it bore a titled lady's name) from one of these charities containing a Little Bible and a pocket chess set. When I returned home my Dad asked me if I had ever received anything from this lady. Apparently the charity told him how generous they were going to be in sending presents, gifts, food etc. to the prisoners, but I never found anybody who received more than a Little Bible and a pocket chess set. My Dad, presumably along with many other parents of POWs, contributed to this charity throughout the war believing I was benefiting. I don't know what he gave, but have no doubt it involved a certain amount of expense he could ill afford, and was obviously a total 'rip off'. Unfortunately this was only one of many rackets in which some people became involved during the war years. We did not enjoy such luxuries from the Austin, but a lot of chaps received regular packets of cigarettes from factories where they worked.

Gren proudly sporting his 'home-made' collar and tie.

These were welcomed with open arms as a useful source of buying or bartering, and many were willing to forfeit their portion of bread for a couple of cigarettes.

During the time I had at my disposal whilst swinging the lead in sickbay, I decided to be the first in the camp to sport a shirt with a collar. Officers had collars to their shirts but in the 1940s army shirts for the ordinary ranks finished at the neckband. As our tunics buttoned right up to the neck a collar was thought unnecessary. I decided I would like a collar so made one from the tail of my shirt and then found a piece of lighter Khaki material with which I made a tie.

We had some very clever chaps in the camp, as well as rogues, vagabonds, and millionaires. One worked marvellous embroidery and for a few fags would embroider a regimental badge, which people put on their shirts. Others could make very good lanyards out of a piece of string. Gordon Rolls from the millionaire family of Rolls Razors was with us, together with a chap from the family of Colman's Mustard. When I was in sickbay I became friendly with William Shergold Worth, from The House of Worth, couturiers. There were also many very well educated people and some brilliant musicians, one who still performs at reunions to this day. Some officers were based down in the town of Marienburg, from where the administration for the camp was controlled. All parcels and mail for the prisoners were received there and then brought up to the camp (if the authorities thought fit) though we were well aware that not all parcels got through. Sometimes they were held back as punishment for some misdemeanour, but we had no way of knowing how many parcels we were denied. Staff from our main camp went down there every day to carry out various duties, and occasionally managed to glean snippets of news from the front which they passed to a POW named Sam. Sam, who was a reader for Reynolds News, wore small, thick spectacles and suffered agonies from boils. When he had news he called us all to the washroom, on his return to camp, to relay the information. Initially we had a propaganda news-sheet issued to us in English by the Germans, which told us how badly Britain was doing. It proudly reported how much shipping or aircraft we'd lost only for this to be countered by the allies with, "We never had that much in the first place". Consequently that soon frittered out.

After I returned from working on a farm a wind-up gramophone, with a handful of records, had appeared in camp (I have no idea where from but presumably the consequence of some bartering). The camp favourite was Bing Crosby and Francis Langford singing 'Gypsy Sweetheart', which used to be played time and time again. Another favourite was 'Piccolo Pete'.

To my knowledge there was no Escape Committee in Stalag XXB but a few attempts at escaping were made. Ivanhoe Austin Gandy, who was a very disruptive fellow, was one of the prime movers in the escapes. (Some time after the war I went to Darlaston on business and, whilst there, tried to locate Ivan, but there was no mention of the name Gandy in any Directory. Interestingly, whilst doing research for this book, I also failed to find any trace of Gandy's name in the lists of Prisoners of War.) In camps where tunnels were dug the prisoners were confined, never leaving their camp in the way we did, so with ours being a working camp, if anyone wanted to escape it was best to do as the Airforce Officers had done and join a working party.

Having said that most of the chaps tried their hardest to avoid work, and I certainly had no wish to help the German cause by working. But eventually fate turned his hand against me. Having spent virtually all of 1941 'playing sick', it was just prior to Christmas that the Germans decided to sort us out, and instead of leaving it to the British Authorities they sent *their* doctors in to identify malingerers. First priority was to get rid of people out of sickbay and although I still had a gammy leg this did not necessitate my staying in there. A hut was set aside for the 'walking wounded' into which we were put and given a card, different coloured cards signifying different criteria. There were two types of card – 'Excused Duty', which was the prime one people went for, and 'Light Duties'. I was issued with an 'Excused Duty' because I made out I was in a terrible state and could hardly walk. Every time I put weight on my leg the wound opened up again.

Christmas was now looming so it was decided to forfeit part of our rations for a period of weeks beforehand so that, instead of the inevitable soup, we could have a 'dry' dinner for Christmas Day – a bit of potato, swede, turnip etc. This, together with items from Red Cross parcels, which we were receiving fairly regularly at this stage, would make the Day slightly more bearable. On Christmas Eve a group of Russian prisoners were brought into the camp who, unfortunately, were discovered to be carrying typhus. This necessitated immediate action, and as Willenberg did not have a plant of its own at that time, resulted in the entire camp having to be escorted to Marienburg, starting on Christmas Day, to be deloused. Groups of men were despatched at intervals, the first group to leave being the hospital patients, the only group for whom transport was laid on. The 'Excused Duties' were the second group, and by no means a fit bunch of fellows. Just as my group had collected our Christmas dinners, the order came for us to leave everything, set off and we were told we could have our meal when we returned. Marienburg was five miles away, and we now had to traverse the journey on foot, poorly equipped with light clothing and ill-fitting footwear. Deep snow already covered the ground, the weather was bitterly cold, and we became increasingly more demoralised with each step as, thoroughly miserable, freezing cold, wet through and without any feeling in either hands or feet, we battled against strong winds and driving snow that cut into one's face. The delousing session was an extremely traumatic affair. Firstly we were ordered to strip off all our clothes, and whilst we stood around naked, these were put on hangers into ovens, which, by our reckoning, far from killing the lice as intended, simply hatched out more than went in. It aroused all the eggs that had been laid and were lying dormant in the seams of shirts and trousers and all the other nooks and crannies, where they had been secreted to await the warmth that spurred them into action. When we re-dressed, these lice, which had not taken kindly to being awoken from their slumbers, raced to the nearest piece of flesh they could find to inflict their wrath on our emaciated and miserable bodies. The resultant itching and soreness, not to mention the physical drain on those already very weak and traumatised, sometimes became unbearable. As a very unfit bunch it took us a long time to trudge the five miles there, go through the delousing process and trudge the five miles back. It was pitch dark long before we reached camp and the Christmas concert, which had been scheduled to take place that night, was just ending. To add to our misery, during our absence the camp officials, in their wisdom and malice, had decided to fumigate the hut, with our dinners and goodies from Red Cross parcels still inside, rendering everything inedible. No food, no concert, frozen solid and more lice than we began with – a 'not to be forgotten' Happy Christmas!

Marienburg – Stalag XXB. Another Welsh group. Gren is second from left in the front row. In the middle of the front row is the smallest militiaman in the British Army at that time.

7

FORCED LABOUR WORK PARTIES

T
ime wended its slow, monotonous way by until the day came when, despite my protestations, I was pronounced fit and ready for work and so, on Easter Sunday 1942 twenty of us were sent to the farming community of Schönau where we were housed in a single storey wooden building, which was divided into four sections. Each section comprised one room big enough for four double bunks and a table, and a smaller room, which took one single bunk leaving no room for anything else. In the entrance was a stove with a copper boiler under which, to our complete delight, a fire could be lit to obtain the luxury of hot water.

Marienburg, May 1941. Gren, front row left, sporting a crew cut and a pair of 'home-made' sandals; two pieces of wood with a strip of leather over the top. On Gren's left Ray Allbrow.

The main room had a heating facility built of brick, with a tower of ceramic tiles rising up to the ceiling, which radiated heat into the room. The aperture for the fire was really quite small. The first section housed a German family, an elderly couple with their son, daughter-in-law and their child. The next housed a Polish family, husband and wife with five or six children, then we had the next two with ten of us in each area. Our section was separated from the families with barbed wire fencing. Outside was a wooden hut in which metal cans were provided for use as a latrine. The building belonged to a chap called Regier who owned the biggest farm in the village. Having dumped our bits and pieces we were paraded up to the first farm at the far end of the village where the guard in charge instructed Ernie, who was standing next to me and spoke a smattering of German, and me, who spoke no German at all, to work. The person in charge of the farm, whose surname was Licfett, was an elderly Prussian man who walked with the aid of a stick, had white hair and a Kaiser Bill moustache. His wife was a large, typical German Haus Frau. Three people, drafted in by the Authorities at the beginning of the war, and who had slightly more freedom than we were allowed, were already working on the farm: Stanislava (known as Sacha) Lemski, a Polish girl who worked primarily in the house, cooking and cleaning, Agnes Levinski, another Polish girl, who was the milkmaid, (she was a very pretty girl who came from a farming fraternity but unfortunately a cow had stood on her foot when she was a little girl, leaving her with a permanently deformed foot), and a Ukranian farmer, Stefan Nakenechski, all of whom were slightly older than me.

Ernie, who was in the Medical Corps, advocated that in civilian life he was valet to a Harley Street specialist – a titled gentleman – Sir De La Jefferson. Licfett decided he was to be called Ernst, and being totally unable to get his tongue round my name decided I should be called Max. The couple had a daughter who lived in an adjacent village, a son in the army as an ordinary soldier and a son who was an SS man, all of whom we met in due course.

Apparently possession of the farm had passed to Licfett through a very sad state of affairs. Two bachelor brothers, his nephews, originally owned the property and when the first one received his 'call-up' papers for the German Army, having no wish to join, he went into the barn and hanged himself. A short time later the other nephew received *his* 'call-up' papers, but also having no desire to join the German army took his life in the same way. Licfett, who was a market gardener, had been a reasonably wealthy man in his time, but having frittered all his money away, was given the responsibility of running the farm. He wasn't a likeable man at all and because he had two sons in the forces was exceedingly unfriendly towards we Brits.

One of his sons had a girlfriend who came from Cologne. He came home on leave several times while I worked there and, on a couple of occasions, his girlfriend came to stay at the farm for a holiday. He seemed a very nice chap and she too was very friendly often coming to chat with me. On her second visit she came alone, but since her previous visit they had become engaged, and when she alighted from the bus, which stopped outside the farm, Licfett and Frau were there to welcome her. She put her bags down, and seeing me in the yard left them with her luggage whilst, in great excitement, she rushed straight over to show me her engagement ring.

By now it was becoming apparent that it would be advantageous for me to learn some German. Basically all I knew was 'brot' (for bread) and 'nicht verstehen' (I don't understand) which had held me in good stead up to that point as by the time others had shown me how to do things several times (against my protestations of not understanding) the job was complete. However, I began to realise that Ernie's minimal knowledge of the language was getting us into trouble. Licfett, knowing that I understood very little of the language, gave instructions to Ernie who always answered, "Ja, ja, ja". One day, as I was cutting beet for the cattle, Licfett was talking to him and pointing in a certain direction. The only word I understood was 'kette' meaning chain. Ernie, who obviously had not understood any better than me, went off to find a chain. He was away for some time, during which Licfett kept appearing and asking where he was. Eventually Ernie returned with a piece of chain, which, unfortunately, was not to Licfett's liking, and he protested vehemently, hurling mouthfuls of abuse at him. We went through the same rigmarole again and he went off for the second time, this time staying away for considerably longer than the first whilst Licfett became increasingly more agitated. Eventually, having traipsed round all the local fields he returned with a huge chain, which fortunately was the correct one and was needed to attach the plough.

Some time later, when we were sewing seed, we were using two horses side by side to drag the sewing machine which followed on behind with Stefan controlling the flow of seed. I was astride one horse whilst attempting to control both when Licfett appeared and began ranting and railing at me. Not understanding what he was shouting about I thought perhaps I was going too fast so gradually slowed to a snail's pace. However, the slower I went the more angry he became and it transpired he was telling me to go faster. It was now obvious that Ernie's scanty knowledge of German was far more likely to be a hindrance than a help and would probably get us into serious trouble, so I decided I'd better make an attempt to learn the language.

Prisoners were spread all around the area working on various farms and together we very quickly all agreed to seize every available opportunity to steal what food we could lay our hands on. *We* found some potatoes, some others managed to get a few eggs, but the piéce de resistance was discovered by a Welshman who came back to base with a sack over his shoulder containing ½ cwt of peas. The peas were a golden brown colour and made the very acceptable soup served in the main camp on rare occasions, and which everyone agreed was a real treat – the only thing we looked forward to. We hid the sack of peas in the stove, where there was just enough room to squash them in behind the ceramic tiles. We had a pot in which we could do our own cooking so with great relish we made ourselves pea soup day after day until we reached the stage where we became heartily sick of it and none of us wanted to see pea soup ever again.

Our first guard on this farm, Jungblud, came from Cologne. He was anti-Nazi, and a very nice, friendly chap, who frequently talked to us telling us all sorts of tales of woe about the bombing of his city. One day I got hold of a Red Cross parcel box and filled it with peas. The following morning, being the last to leave for work, I asked him if he would like a box. He declined the offer so I informed him it was a good, strong box and suggested he might want to send something home to his wife at sometime. Agreeing that was a good idea he went to pick it up, looked somewhat startled at the weight, slid the lid off and upon perceiving the contents his eyes lit up in delight. From then on we had him exactly where we wanted him. He'd arrive in the morning, chop sticks with his bayonet, light the fire and get the pot boiling before he ousted us from our beds. He was a fantastic guy but one day arrived in a great state of distress telling us he was being posted to the Russian Front.

Four of our boys worked for Regier, the wealthiest man in the district, from whom they 'acquired' a milk churn. Another four chaps worked at another farm and they also acquired a milk churn. Each morning when the men went to Regier's, their first job was to load the milk churns onto a cart and bring them down to the roadside to be collected. Whilst doing this they filled the two empty churns with water, which we took back to our shed and used for washing, cooking, making drinks etc. with any surplus being poured into the boiler. On Saturday, as I was invariably the first back I lit the fire under the boiler and as the chaps returned they would book themselves in. I would be first and used the warmed water, which filled a bowl approximately eighteen inches in diameter and to a comparable depth, to wash to the waist, followed by the next nine in turn, all using the same water. Following this, and again using the same water, we each took it in turns to stand in it and wash our lower half. Next all the clothes went in and they were washed. Then the sludge that was left was used to wash the table and wipe the floor; the moral of the day being 'waste not want not'.

We worked six days a week and were each fed on our individual farms. From my point of view this was advantageous as on our small farm they couldn't be bothered to make anything 'special' (i.e. inferior) for we prisoners so we had virtually the same food as the farmer but less in quantity and of a poorer standard, ours being watered down and made with milk from which the cream had been extracted. However, this was considerably better than the swill we had received in the main camps. Sacha filled my army water bottle with milk every day and hid it in the barn for me to collect on the way out. So basically at this stage we fared reasonably well.

At one point both Sacha and Agnes were in the field loading a cart with hay. Stefan brought the loaded cart down to the barn and then threw the hay up into the loft, Ernie moved the hay from the loft to Licfett, Licfett moved it to me and I was delegated to stack it at the back of the barn. Frequently Licfett berated Ernie for not putting the hay on the correct spot – he just chucked it anywhere, which meant Licfett had to move. This increasingly aggravated him until in a livid rage he lashed out with his pitchfork. Ernie parried it with his own pitchfork then made out that he had been hit, although we both knew he hadn't, but I was not going to stand for this, so we immediately downed tools and I sent him off to fetch the guard. He went down into the byre where horses were kept in one area, cows were milked in another and there were about four sheep in a pen. The gangway between these areas couldn't have been more than three feet. All of a sudden such a hue and cry arose as Agnes yelled out, "Max, Max". I went down to discover Ernie, whose height was six feet plus, collapsed on the floor. Within this confined space he had neither hit his head nor hurt himself, but was lying in a prone position moaning, groaning and faking concussion. Playing the same game I naturally made a terrific song and dance about this and the old man appeared quaking with fear thinking he'd killed Ernie. The Frau appeared looking terrified and panicking as I expostulated that Licfett was not safe to be about and should be locked up. I requested water for the patient to drink, mopped his brow and we generally made as much drama as we possibly could. Eventually I managed to get him up and said, "That's it, we're going", and we set off back to our quarters. After a short distance I became aware that Ernie was leaning very heavily on me, acting it out to the limit and thoroughly enjoying every minute of it, whereupon I impolitely suggested he packed it in as we were beyond their view and out of sight. After this little incident the authorities decided to reduce the party by half, Ernie was sent back to Marienburg, and Maurice, a chap from another farm, came to work with me.

Licfett's son who was in the SS and had been wounded at the Russian Front, came home on leave. We were harvesting Rape at the time and because the seed is so small this necessitated lining the carts with tarpaulins. One of us on the ground threw the sheaves up to the other who stood on the cart making sure the heads of the sheaves pointed inwards so that all the seed dropped into the tarpaulin. Stefan then took away the loaded cart and left us an empty one. No one was supervising so we were taking things nice and leisurely when, out of the blue, the son arrived very disgruntled at the way we were doing the job. He began hurling abuse at us and telling us to go faster, and when the next empty cart appeared he jumped onto it saying he would show us how to do the job properly. At this point Maurice and I decided if that was what he wanted that was what he would have! Sheaves were stacked in a long line with the cart going down the middle, and with Maurice on one side and me on the other we both went into overdrive and began throwing sheaves at him left, right and centre. Struggling to keep up he was even more disgruntled at this and instead of telling us to get a move on he was now bawling at us to go slower. When the cart was loaded he took it away and was never seen again.

Periodically we worked with the sugar beet – making drills, planting the seeds and thinning the plants out. The Polish worked hard but we had no intention of doing any more than was absolutely necessary. At certain intervals along the drills we were required to leave a little cluster of plants. We were quite happy to do this but in our own time, i.e. as slowly as possible, whereas Agnes was quite the opposite and worked as fast as she could. She would be down a row and well on her way back up the next before we'd reached the quarter-way point, which considerably irked Licfett. Having done that we then, with a short handled dibber, planted one single plant at intervals. At this I was even slower whereas Agnes again was as quick as lightning. Licfett and I were always having words, and one day when I was sitting down to perform this task, Agnes was working somewhere behind me. Licfett came out and obviously objected to me doing my work in such a leisurely fashion. Suddenly Agnes shouted, "Watch out Max". I turned round to see Licfett brandishing a stick with which he was about to hit me. As I turned round he left me and went to Agnes raising the stick to hit her. I intervened and saved her a beating, but that night she ran away. She could have been in serious trouble for warning me, and even more serious trouble had she been caught whilst absconding, but we heard later that she went some distance away and ended up working for the local Burgermeister, which turned out to be a much better job.

We were one of the very few farms allowed to have a bull and local farmers brought their cows to us to be served. On these occasions my services were always required to help with the process. We tied a rope round the horns of the cow, placed a tuft of hay on top of her head to prevent the rope burning, threaded the rope through the spokes of the cartwheel and the person who owned the cow then stood on the cart and held the rope to keep her steady. Following this I fetched the bull, leading it by a rope clipped onto the ring through its nose. Licfett, who had always been there to officiate, happened to be away one day when a cow arrived. The farmer had come some distance and insisted the cow had to be served there and then. Fancying I was equal to the task I took the onus upon myself to organise the deed, but because of my inexperience the poor bull ended up unable to get any satisfaction as the cow kept moving her rump. In between each attempt I had to walk the bull round to recharge his batteries! By the time the farmer left his cow was satisfied, but my old Licfett wasn't. He returned home to a totally exhausted bull, which he insisted I'd almost killed!

Once a man came to the farm to slaughter a pig, obviously an underhand operation as no animal was supposed to be slaughtered without permission from the authorities. He arrived with a humane killer and the deed took place in the barn, away from prying eyes. A pistol containing a bolt was put against the animal's forehead, the trigger was pulled and a spike entered the head piercing the brain. The pig's throat was then slit

Another 'official' photo. Gren, third from left middle row, with a group of his POW colleagues in Marienburg in 1941 in 'summer wear'! with Ray Allbrow on his right.

73

and the girls stood ready with large bowls to catch the blood, which they used to make black pudding. Once the blood had been drained scalding water was thrown over the carcass and then, by scraping it with large bells (like Swiss cow bells) we removed all the bristles. Following this the slaughter-man cut the carcass into joints. The Frau was constantly back and forth keeping an eye on things and suddenly became aware that a large ham had been put to one side. She was about to pick this up when a huge hand descended upon her shoulder and the slaughter-man told her, in no uncertain terms, that was his. A violent argument passed between them, but he made it perfectly clear that was his share of the booty and nobody was going to deprive him of it. This was his perk in addition to his fee, and she had no alternative but to very grudgingly concede.

In the farming community in which we now lived everybody owned different things which were shared between all the farms in the area. My farm was comparatively small, and in addition to the bull which served the local community's cows, we also owned a threshing machine. Periodically the Military arrived to assess what each owner possessed. On one visit they told us our bull was past its 'sell-by' date so they took it away and we were issued with a replacement. We had four horses, all of which were old-timers. The nicest looking one, which happened to be the oldest of the lot, was not used as a working horse; he was a show horse and Licfett used him to pull his trap. Sometimes I was detailed to saddle up this horse and take something to his daughter who lived in another village. I was no horseman and kept falling off if the beast trotted, but funnily enough was able to stay mounted when it galloped. Everybody owned a few horses but Helmut Regier, the man on whose land we were situated, had a huge farm and excellent livestock. His older brother had been running a smaller adjacent farm and when Helmut was called up this brother was drafted in to control both farms. Two of our boys worked on the smaller farm but were removed when the brother became vicious towards them and started roughing them up. Rumours abounded as to why Regier, a comparatively young man, had not been drafted into the forces. On assessment visits, if the Military found decent horses, they removed them for Army use, but it became very noticeable that Regier's were never taken. He always accommodated the Officers for the night, and no doubt wined and dined them, which seemed to do the trick, until one day something went awry and he did get called up. He was a very good horseman and taught our boys who went to work for him to ride bareback and, very surprisingly, even gave them embrocation to rub into their backsides when they became chaffed.

On one occasion Stefan and I were delegated to travel to a particular spot to pick up the farm's allocation of a year's supply of coal. We took a cart and were virtually the last to arrive. The Burgermeister who was marching up and down the line of waiting carts organising everything, suggested everybody helped everybody else. This was fine by us but we soon became aware that fair play was not being acted upon and as each cart filled up so that cart and driver left. This meant that Stefan and I, having helped load everybody else's carts, were the only ones left when the time came to load ours, a fact about which we were not best pleased.

Some time later we were despatched to the same place, with two carts this time, to collect our allocation of logs. Maurice and I took one cart and Stefan took the other. Still smarting from the previous experience I suggested to Maurice and Stefan that we refused to help anybody else and only loaded our own. As before when we reached our pick-up point we were virtually at the back of the queue. The Burgermeister was again shouting, "Everybody helps everybody". Stefan decided he would help but Maurice and I made it perfectly clear that we were not prepared to help anybody and did not expect anybody to help us. The logs, which were all of a similar length, were on the side of a railway track and had to be loaded into a cradle, which looked rather like an upside down table with four 'legs' sticking up at each corner. This gave a specific allocation, but it was an arduous task loading them into the cradle to reach the required measure and then having to lift them out again to load onto the cart. It worked exactly as before with each cart being driven off immediately it was filled. Just as we were about to start loading our carts two elderly men joined the end of the queue announcing that they would help us if we would then help them, but were extremely puzzled when Maurice and I declined the offer. Having loaded our quota we set off on our return journey and, because we were running late, were racing the horses. Obviously we became a bit too enthusiastic to reach base for at one point the cart tilted sharply and because we had thrown the logs in in a willy nilly fashion instead of stacking them correctly, they all fell off and rolled into a ditch. To avoid the embarrassment of someone coming along and witnessing our plight we then had to work like fury to reload the logs. Fortunately no one came along and our bigheaded stupidity was never found out.

The Burgermeister, who lived at the far end of the village from where we were billeted, was the only person in the village who possessed a boar so when our sows were ready for serving I was duly despatched to fetch the animal. It was massive and could have pulled me anywhere it felt inclined. A rope was tied round one of its hind legs and, having been given strict instructions by the Burgermeister not to race it, I set off back to base. I had no intention whatsoever of racing the animal and was very happy wandering along letting it grub about in the hedges and ditches to its heart's content. As expected, upon my return I was greeted by the wrath of Licfett for having been gone far too long. He was adamant I should have come at greater speed, despite my protestations that the Burgermeister had insisted I was not to walk the boar at a fast pace. We kept it for a couple of days to perform its duty after which I was sent on the return journey with strict instructions to be quick about it.

On our farm there was a German shepherd dog called Zepple, a very tolerant, patient and well-behaved bitch who, apart from being taken out to bring in the cattle for milking, spent the remainder of the time tied up. Therefore, much to everyone's surprise, Zepple suddenly produced a litter of seven pups, which did not please Licfett one little bit. He immediately decided the pups had to be drowned, but, unbeknown to him, I managed to rescue one, a lovely little dog who I named Rollo. I didn't take him back to my farm as officially we weren't allowed pets and there would have been ructions from Licfett had I done so. However, we had a decent guard at the time who turned a blind eye to the fact that we had a dog and Rollo was passed round between the boys on each of the different farms for them to take to work in the morning and bring back in the evening. One farmer, who was the dairyman and owned the second biggest farm in the area, became very attached to Rollo and kept telling the fellows who worked on his farm that he would like to have him. Eventually, as I was sent back, Rollo was left with the boys, and I don't know what happened to him in the end. I sincerely hope he was shown kindness, and allowed to last out his days in peace and quiet.

Two illicit photos taken on the farm at Schönau, Easter 1942. Left Gren and Rollo. Right Gren (the tallest) and the boys he worked with who took Rollo out to their farms each day and brought him back at night.

On a lighter side, although I could see perfectly well, to relieve the dreadful monotony I told the guard that my eyes were bad. He obtained permission to take me to see an optician in Danzig (now Gdansk), involving a train journey of approximately one hour. By now my motley uniform was virtually in tatters. Stefan was the proud owner of a beautiful pair of black, highly polished riding boots which he had bought in the Ukraine prior to the war, and which were his pride and joy. He had worked hard for a month to earn a sufficient amount to buy the leather and then another month to be able to afford to have them made. Wishing to look a little more respectable for the outing I managed to persuade Stefan to lend me his boots in exchange for some cigarettes. One of our chaps possessed a new pair of army trousers, which he agreed to lend me, but as I was several inches taller than him they came half way up my calves. However, by pulling the trouser legs over the riding boots I managed to give the impression of a box pleat. Another chap loaned me a decent jacket, I had my own shirt with the collar and tie and a fairly respectable cap loaned by someone else. Compared to how we normally looked, strongly resembling a tramp in our dirty, tatty old clothes, I ended up looking 'top of the range'. When the guard arrived in the morning he looked like a load of rubbish as by this time the guards' uniforms had really gone down the nick. For a long time they'd been issued with grey flannel slacks – not even proper uniform trousers. They still had their green/greyish uniform jackets, but only ordinary flannel trousers, which now were very well worn. On top of that he had to carry a respirator, which was in a metal container, his haversack, a rifle and ammunition – he looked a proper mess. He came in expecting to find the usual ragged pauper but to his amazement and embarrassment was confronted by this immaculately dressed prisoner. He wanted to know how I had acquired the clothes, the boots in particular, so I told him they had arrived in a Red Cross parcel. Off we went on the Klienbahn, a small railway with carriages like the old tramcars and a little engine on the front, and I was highly amused to witness the passengers staring in disbelief at the apparent difference in apparel between the people who were supposed to be winning the war and those believed to be losing. Arriving in Danzig we were making our way to the opticians when along the road appeared Wilf Jackson, one of the original group of four who joined up with me, who was digging a hole at the side of the road. It was the first time I'd seen him for years and we managed to exchange a few words before I was moved on. The optician's name was Schilling. He couldn't speak English and I couldn't speak German – talk about the blind leading the blind! However, he indicated to me to read the chart and knowing that there are some German letters, which are comparable to ours, I managed to fob him off with something. Eventually he decided on a prescription and a week or so later I was presented with a pair of glasses, for which I paid with our useless camp money. To this day I swear they were just plain glass.

Occasionally we had a decent guard who would try to obtain items for us. I wanted an SS ring to keep as a memento and one guard did his best to get hold of one for me but to no avail.

An adjacent farmer, who was in the Luftwaffe, was allowed special leave to return home for harvesting. As his farm didn't have a threshing machine he borrowed ours and Licfett sent me, the only British chap, along to join the two to three dozen other young lads from several nationalities detailed to work there to gather in the harvest. Just as we were about to begin a farmer pulled up in his cart. He had a young Russian lad with him who only looked about seventeen and seemed scared stiff. He was dressed in his best suit, was carrying a little attaché case and had been brought there straight from the pick up point without any question of being taken to his allotted farm first. We were all issued with our various tasks and a Russian girl and I were given the job of forming the hayrick. When the straw came out of the threshing machine, it ascended an elevator before dropping to the ground. We then had to move the hay across with our pitchfork to form a base, which was dead easy at first, but obviously as the rick rose higher it took increasingly less time to get back to the hay dropping off the elevator. This meant we had to work like the clappers to prevent a huge build up, and it was a really hard day's work. When we finished we were herded into a barn where a table had been set up to feed the workers, and the alleged food was brought out. I was obviously lucky in that I had been better fed than the rest of the group, and as far as I was concerned it was pigswill. The young Russian lad who was sitting opposite to me was so hungry he attacked the food in an avaricious way, shovelling it down as quickly as possible. I offered him my share, which he took and consumed equally rapidly. A minute portion of a sweet followed the swill, something like semolina, but made with milk that had been skimmed to little more than water. That was equally horrible so I gave that to the lad too. I then left and as I came through the barn passed the man from the Luftwaffe and one or two other farmers who had come to collect their people. The farmer called, "See you tomorrow Englander?" In rather impolite German, interspersed with good old Anglo Saxon swear words, I replied in no uncertain terms that I was not prepared to flog myself to death again to be rewarded with food barely fit for pigs to eat! On returning to my farm to collect my jacket I met Licfett in the yard. He said, "Alright Max?" I said, "No, I'm not going back there again". "Why not?" he queried. I told him, "We slaved away all day only to be given pigswill to eat". To my absolute amazement he put his arm on my shoulder and said, "Come", then took me in and gave me a meal. Normally we were at loggerheads with each other and that was the first bit of kindness he'd ever shown towards me.

Whilst at the farm I had been delegated official barber. Living locally on Regier's land were two Russian girls plus a Russian family of six. One of the girls, Anna, who was about eighteen, had shoulder length hair which she had grown weary of so asked me if I would cut it. I explained I'd never cut a girl's hair in my life. However, after some persuasion I went to the farm one Sunday morning to cut her hair. It took me ages, as I was very fastidious about doing it. She had extremely strong hair, which kept springing away from the scissors, and I had great difficulty in getting it level. Fortunately, when I had finished she was delighted with my efforts and informed me I'd cut it just how she wanted.

8

TRIAL, RETRIBUTION
AND THE REICHBAHN PARTY

In early spring the cattle were put out into the meadow and, as they became acclimatised to eating the fresh grass, produced an abundance of milk. At the time when the milk was so free flowing the cattle belonging to Regier's farm were in a field opposite to where we were living. My mate Jim Stewart, a Scot who suffered from stomach ulcers, found it very difficult to rest and invariably was the first person to be up and about in a morning boiling water for a drink. At this period we had an Assistant Guard, an elderly German who lived in the block in which we lived. He was issued with an armband and given a set of keys so that if the guard was detained he could come down and open the gate to enable us to go to work early, if we felt so inclined (which was very optimistic of them!). One morning, as I was still lounging in my bunk, Jim was having a wash in the kitchen area when I became aware of a terrific commotion going on. When he came out, he said Regier's brother had appeared, thrown the water out of one of our milk churns and taken it away. I told him he shouldn't have allowed him to do so. Following this I was stripped to the waist having a wash when the brother re-appeared on the scene. Having seen our other churn he wanted that too. As I'd told Jim he shouldn't have let him take the first one I now had to defend the second, so I told him he couldn't have it. He started ranting and raving at me and ascended the first of the two steps leading up into the hut. I had no intention of allowing him to enter my 'bathroom' and issued a strong warning informing him that he was forbidden to even enter the perimeter, yet alone the building. He told me he'd do whatever he wanted and climbed up another step. This I resented

81

most strongly so grabbed him by the collar and went to clout him, but when he saw my intention he pulled away and cleared off, leaving me anticipating dire consequences. As I expected he fetched the guard, who at that time, was quite a decent chap. He arrived as we were having our breakfast prior to going to work. As we exchanged 'Good Mornings' and one or two other little pleasantries, I was sitting near the door observing Regier out in the yard. The guard asked who had hit his brother, but having collaborated on the issue, we all denied any knowledge of such a happening. After some further discussion on the matter the guard turned to Regier who pointed me out. I explained I hadn't hit him and gave my version of things, insisting I'd only put my hand out to prevent him entering the building. The guard appeared to accept my explanation and went out to speak to Regier. However, some days later I was told to pack my kit and was sent back to base camp at Willenberg to stand trial.

The trial was held before an officer who accused me of striking the man. I denied this again explaining I'd only put my hand out to restrain him. Considerable discussion took place and all appeared to be going reasonably well until, through sheer frustration, I suggested in German, that the farmer was mad. He took exception to this remark and from then on I realised I'd sealed my fate. I had grabbed Regier's brother's clothing and if he *had* advanced further I believe I would have lashed out at him. He was a horrible man, and, as I mentioned before, had already had two chaps removed from him as he had knocked them about. However, I quite truthfully insisted that I had *not* hit him, but to commit the crime of calling a member of the Third Reich mad was more than sufficient to get me banged up. I was given fourteen days in solitary, but at least I got away from the farm and from Regier.

At times, when there was a backlog awaiting trial, people were detained in a confined area in the main camp. This was simply a hut surrounded by extra barbed wire and called the Straffelager. Having been 'tried, found guilty' and given my sentence I went straight into 'Solitary', a block of cells inside a brick building below the Straffelager. Between each cell was a single layer of bricks in which my predecessors had bored holes in the cement between the layers. There were approximately eighteen individual cells with a small compound outside where we were allowed to stretch our

Official photo taken in the new delousing dept. Gren is second from right, second row from back. However, when the Germans found the photo was so bad they congregated us together again and took another one outside the delouser!

legs for half an hour or so twice a day. Each cell contained a bed made of the usual boards, a blanket, a washing facility and a bucket for a toilet. The loneliness and boredom of being confined entirely on one's own for fourteen days was a demoralising experience. The holes in the pointing enabled prisoners to talk to each other, but primarily were used for passing round cigarettes. Each prisoner was searched prior to being banged up and any cigarettes confiscated, but a number still managed to smuggle some through. The shout would go round, "Anybody got a light?" It always seemed to be the person furthest away from the light who had the cigarette. Next a piece of paper containing the cigarette was fed through the hole in each cell and passed all the way round to the chap who had the light. We didn't have matches but those who smoked invariably had a flint, a razor blade and a celluloid toothbrush, which was highly flammable. Shavings of celluloid were scraped from the toothbrush handle to make a little mound of chippings on a piece of paper, the flint was put into the split end of a piece of wood or pencil and struck until a spark from it ignited the scrapings whereupon the cigarette could then be lit. However, by the time it got back to its original owner everyone had taken a few puffs and the cry would then go up, "Where's me bloody fag gone?" as the owner received the dog end!

Having been on Licfett's farm for a year, when I came out of Solitary I was detailed for another working party. New huts had been built primarily for people who worked locally going out each day and returning to camp each night. They were long huts and very modern with individual rooms plus a washroom – the height of luxury! Each room contained two-tier wooden slatted bunks for about ten men. A delouser was also built, saving the need for our regular ten mile round treks down into Marienburg. One day I bumped into Benny Higgs, who had been in my TA Unit. Benny was a carpenter who had been working in Marienburg for a very long time, and, therefore, had made several useful contacts. He informed me that he knew someone who might be able to get me on the Reichbahn party (the railway party), which was considered to be one of the plum jobs operating out of the main camp. It was a well sought-after job, which, despite the fact that it was very heavy work, had its perks. True to his word, before long the instruction came for me to join the railway party which involved a five mile march to a siding each day where we unloaded an average of seven tons of coal per man per shift. We were split into two shifts one to work mornings and the other afternoons. Upon arrival we took off our uniforms, donned black overalls, then unloaded coal from the trucks onto staging at the side of the track. If the coal was small this necessitated shovelling it out, which made the job considerably more arduous, therefore, we always prayed for large lumps. When the unloading was completed we were allowed to shower to clean off the coal dust before leaving. We only had one guard overseeing us and when he wasn't looking our way we would slip off and inspect all the trucks to see if there was anything in them worth pinching. If there wasn't any coal, which happened occasionally, we were found odd jobs to do, like tidying up, around the yard. That didn't go down very well – nobody wanted to tidy up so a lot of messing about took place. One day the overseer told us there was someone who would give us a lift in a lorry back to camp and we were each to give the driver a cigarette. This began to happen on a regular basis, and before long another driver appeared. The two of them waited to take us back after we had finished our shift and some controversy began to take place as to who had arrived first. Officially we should have been working for eight hours per shift, but we worked hard and finished in half that time. One day, when we arrived for the afternoon shift, the civilian foreman who delegated the work told us somebody had complained about the 'Englanders' knocking off early. We were being paid for doing eight hours work so eight hours it had to be. We all went into a little huddle and agreed our plan of action, informing the foreman we were perfectly willing to do our eight hours. We began throwing out coal at a very leisurely pace when after about six hours, not a lot of progress had been made. The foreman began to get impatient and we were told to hurry up and finish then he and we could knock off. We continued taking our time dragging out the unloading until the eight hours were up and dusk had descended, following which tidying up had to be done and each man had to shower. This lengthened the process considerably, as there were insufficient showers for everybody's use at the same time, so we showered in relays. We dragged these out as long as we could by which time the foreman was livid, the guard was livid and of course the transport was long gone so we then had to march all the way back to camp. It must have been close on midnight when we arrived to be greeted by the equally livid camp Commandant who was unable to leave until he'd locked us in for the night. The next day we were ordered back to our regular routine and no further complaints were received.

Our accommodation was split between three rooms, and an additional perk of the job was that obviously we could purloin coal. Prior to leaving for work each morning we calculated how much coal was needed – maybe two or three bags for the stove in each room which was used for both heating and cooking; and when leaving certain prisoners took a haversack with them. By rotating the men carrying haversacks we then stole sufficient coal to keep a particular room supplied for several days. Sometimes we brought extra coal to give to the guards in order to safeguard our own supply. Obviously the guards knew which party worked where and what contraband they could knock off from the prisoners on return, so when they needed coal two men were deputed to bring theirs back. Came the day when the guards became greedy and decided they wanted all the coal. However they only took the coal we brought on that particular day. Fortunately by this time we had been able to build up a store of coal for ourselves so stopped bringing more, which meant the guards had cut their own throats. After a few days their reserves were gone and as they were getting increasingly more cold and uncomfortable pleaded with us to bring more, and normal service was resumed! We even worked Sundays with half a team enabling us to keep up a constant source of supply.

Another commodity we managed to get hold of was eggs. George Cosgrove, who slept above me, was a really likeable young cockney lad who had been a barrow boy. He never let himself go, as did some other chaps but was always spick and span. He was the egg baron and managed to get hundreds of eggs, bringing them all back in his battledress blouse. He'd trade these in camp for pullovers or socks or anything that was going and would then barter with the civilians and come back with more eggs. When we arrived back at camp we were always checked by the guards for contraband. Some were pretty vicious and when they knew someone had eggs, with a spiteful laugh, would swipe that person across the chest, smashing the eggs. This was invariably done from behind, but once in the know a prisoner would have a couple of cigarettes held up in his hand, which the guard would usually take letting the prisoner pass with eggs intact.

Beyond our hut were the toilets and one very hot summer day, when Cosgrove and I were the only two in the hut, we had all the windows open. I was lying on my bunk and he wanted to cook some eggs but couldn't find the frying pan. He was standing by the stove, which was in a corner with a bunk in front of it, ranting and raving, "Where's the B......... frying pan?" Out of the corner of my eye I saw Captain King, the C/E Padre passing the window on his way to the toilet. He must have heard the blaspheming because he stopped. Seeing this I called, "What did you say Cosgrove?" The colourful expletives were repeated as Cosgrove once again gave vent to his frustrated emotions, followed by the shocked call, "Cosgrove" from the Padre. Cosgrove appeared as red as a beetroot!

As we marched to the railway siding each day we passed a little piece of land, which had been cultivated by one of the civilians and on which was a marrow plant. I jealously watched the marrow growing day by day and came the day, although it wasn't all that big, when I could wait no longer. Much to the annoyance of everyone else, as it turned out all the prisoners had had their eyes on it, I took it. The cry went up from everyone, "Whose pinched my marrow?" Fortunately for me I got in first and savoured every mouthful. I can still taste it to this day it was so delicious.

We had some interesting characters on the Reichbahn party, one being 'Buster' Riker who lived in Brighton and who I tried to locate when visiting there about two years ago, but without any success. I don't know what he did for a living but he was an all-in wrestler and would sometimes put on demonstrations in the camp. I was always amazed to see, for a man of such muscular physique, how extremely artistic he could be. When it became necessary to paint numbers, messages or signs on trucks, such as 'No coal today' Riker was always ordered to do it, which he did in an extremely professional manner.

9

SUGAR FACTORY

Unfortunately all good things come to an end and one evening, in the autumn of 1943, upon returning to camp, we found the entire party was to be included in a group of approximately one hundred chaps who were told to pack up their meagre belongings because the following morning they were being despatched to Altfelde to work in a sugar factory. We arrived at the factory to find we would be working with a small group of POWs who had been there quite some time, and a skeleton staff of civilians. Suddenly a POW who recognised me from way back somewhere approached and said, "When they ask for painters and decorators step forward and you'll be able to come with me". Specialists in particular spheres were duly sought, and when the request was made for a painter and decorator, I did as I'd been told, and was sent to work with the man who, it turned out, was a painter and decorator in Civvy Street. I helped him decorate houses belonging to the sugar factory in which the civilian workers lived, during which time he taught me a lot about the profession.

After approximately two weeks the sugar beet began to arrive and we were then needed to work in the factory. We worked two 12-hour shifts without a break (6am to 6pm and 6pm to 6am) from Monday to Saturday. At weekends we worked from 6pm Saturday evening until midday Sunday, an 18-hour shift without a break, following which the steam had to be cut off for ten minutes for safety reasons. During these ten minutes the shift changed over and the next group worked from midday Sunday to 6am Monday morning, which meant the only time the majority of us saw daylight was during the changeover at midday on Sunday. These shifts applied to everybody, the POWs, who were the mainstay of the workers, the civilians who were few in number, the manager and two female chemists.

Many of the factory jobs were very arduous. We had what was known as the Schlamm Presses, which consisted of hessian attached to a series of metal frames. When the beet had been cut up and mangled the pulp was then manually forced through the presses to extract the juice. It was stiflingly hot in the pressroom and after the pulp had been squeezed through the hessian the presses were opened up, releasing even more heat. The workers, with blunt, machete type knives, scraped off the pressed beet before re-assembling the presses. Because of the intense heat the men only wore shorts and a pair of clogs and whenever possible sneaked out on to a balcony to get some fresh air. Owing to the heat, heaviness of the work, and malnutrition, two workers died during the short while I was there.

Some jobs, such as constantly shovelling in the beet, were extremely strenuous whilst others were demoralisingly tedious. The factory was blacked out and I remember one worker sitting in the gloom by a tower, which rose to the floor above. The tower had a glass window in it across which was a white mark and from wherever the beet was chopped it came down the tower. For twelve hours the fellow sat watching this mark and, if the beet level dropped below it, had to bang some pipes with a lump of wood to tell the chaps at the other end to get a move on and supply more beet.

We lived in a big wooden building inside the factory complex, but many POWs made token escapes simply in order to be caught outside the factory grounds when they would be sent back to the main camp to spend fourteen days in the Bunker (solitary). Upon release they were not returned to the factory but were posted to different jobs, which was infinitely preferable to many of the jobs and appalling working conditions within the factory.

I have no idea why, but I was chosen to work in the laboratory as assistant to the younger of the two chemists who was a tall well built German, a horrible woman very dictatorial in her attitude. She was a munitions expert who, twelve months previously had volunteered to work in the sugar factory. However, having sampled the work for the season, and finding that 12-hour shifts didn't appeal to her, she decided not to return. Unfortunately she was detailed to return and, having been forced to stay, subsequently carried an air of resentment on her shoulders. She was an out and out Nazi, and absolutely hated the British. The explosives she had worked with had somehow caused damage to the veins in her nose and she permanently kept beside her a large sweet jar full of cotton wool balls to stem the flow of blood from the frequent violent nosebleeds she suffered. These rarely happened on a day shift but were very common at night, when she was often sent home leaving us with the manager in charge carrying out her duties. I was lucky as my job primarily was cleaning utensils and collecting samples, a rather cushy job really. At the beginning of the shift I had to obtain a comprehensive selection of samples from the entire factory. The chemist took what she wanted and analysed the samples, which were from the sugar beet in all its different stages of processing. Throughout the remainder of the shift I was then responsible for obtaining random collections at regular intervals, some hourly, some only twice during the shift. The chemist analysed these further samples and took the results to discuss with the manager in his office. It then befell me to wash all the equipment and utensils she had used. The atmosphere was very sticky as sugar hung in the air and no one seemed to appreciate the amount of sugar that was in the hot water system. Not until the manager came to take over in the laboratory and reprimanded me for not washing the equipment thoroughly did this fact come to light. The equipment, and even the workers who showered in the factory, were coated in sugar after using hot water, and the only way to get rid of it was to wash again in cold water.

Because of the freedom my job afforded me I was able to walk around, talk to people and take over their jobs for a short while, much to their relief as no time off was officially allowed, even to visit the toilet. A canteen was provided for the German guards to which I was sent to fetch meals for the chemist and the manager. Before long the Germans began to suspect that somehow I was involved in the numerous escapes taking place. This was totally untrue; I had no knowledge of who was about to escape although the manager, who seemed a fairly decent chap to me, frequently asked me who was going out that night as he would need to arrange cover for them in order to complete the job. I believe the guards became aware of this, which prompted them into thinking that, because of my freedom, I had something to do with the escapes.

We had all been supplied with white trousers and jackets, but as it was extremely warm in the factory I invariably left my jacket off. On the leg of the trousers and the back of the jacket a black triangle was painted and the breast pocket of the jacket bore our factory number – I was No. 71. One day a guard came up to me in the laboratory wanting to know why I was not wearing my jacket and demanding to know my number. The unpleasant chemist, who was in a particularly foul mood that day, told me to throw him out. I declined to do this and gave him my number. Later she went to the manager to protest about the interference of the guards coming into her laboratory; but it made no difference, they still came to check up on us at regular intervals. As I had to work with her I did try to be friendly and bribed her with a piece of chocolate, all to no avail, she continued to be horrible. The chemist on the other shift was very nice and the POW who worked with her got on extremely well. With my unlimited resources of

Photo sent to Gren by his brother in June 1944 showing Derek dressed entirely in Gren's clothes, green trousers, sports jacket and salmon coloured shirt.

travel round the factory I was one of the few POWs allowed to enter the place where the sugar was loaded into sacks ready to be sent away. A civilian guard was placed permanently outside the sugar store to discourage stealing. It was very seldom that samples of the finished product were needed in the laboratory, and the advantage of this soon became apparent to me. When the chemist departed to have supper with the manager I took a couple of containers and told the guard we needed samples for the laboratory. I filled my containers and made off with them to be used later for bartering.

Because of the suspicions that I was somehow involved in the escapes it seemed that, after a while, my every move was being watched and one blustery evening when going to collect the meals, I (a non-smoker) suddenly fancied a cigarette. I always carried some with me in case an opportunity arose for bartering. I stepped outside the factory where the strong wind defeated my attempt to light up, so went back inside where a guard spotted me and I was duly reported for smoking in a forbidden area. Yet again I was sent for the mandatory fourteen days in Solitary. It was now winter and extremely cold so my spell this time was very miserable and uncomfortable.

Upon my release the sugar factory party had returned so I was sent to resume my coal heaving duties on the Reichbahn.

10

RETURN TO MARIENBURG

One day we had a visit from a recruitment agency. A chap, who had been in Stalag XXB for some time, was in the Queen Victoria Rifles and was allegedly secretary to Sir Oswald Moseley. He arrived, with two others, in a German Army Officer's uniform in an attempt to enlist people to join the British Free Forces. Their aim was to recruit the Irish, who were presumed to hate the British, then the Welsh and Scots, leaving the English until last, by which time they hoped to have enlisted a whole Battalion. All Irishmen were invited to a meeting where it was explained that if they became members, together with all the other advantages of joining the BFF, they wouldn't have to fight the British but could vent their spleen on the Russians. However, apparently the Irish were not to be persuaded, and things did not work out quite as the agency anticipated, no one wishing to volunteer to become their cannon fodder. The Irish gave the instigators such a rough ride the meeting was soon abandoned, they were sent away without signing up one conscript and were never heard of again.

One of our lads, whose surname was Carroll, and who was working on a large farm decided he had had enough. After mulling over a plan of campaign, whilst working out in the fields one day, before all the other farm workers of both sexes, he stripped off and started running around the field stark naked. The guards caught him and sent him back to camp where he was assessed by a doctor and diagnosed as mentally deranged. Actually he was perfectly sane; this was simply a ploy he persevered with for days and weeks to come. To fool the camp guards into believing he was a lunatic, he acquired a little wooden horse, which he trailed behind him all round the perimeter fencing at regular intervals during the day. Once he'd completed his rounds he would then rejoin the boys playing cards and doing whatever else he could to while away the long dreary hours whilst behaving perfectly normally. The time came when the Germans decided to repatriate prisoners who were no longer of any use to the Third Reich (i.e. seriously wounded, ill etc; people such as a Lance Corporal from Lincolnshire who had been taken prisoner in Norway. He'd been badly wounded, and although he could get around he wasn't able to work). A delegation arrived from Switzerland to vet those regarded as unsuitable and to issue permits for them to be sent home, Carroll being amongst those sent for interview. He told us that when they had finished assessing him they gave him a piece of paper telling him that was his permit to go home. At this point, to prove he was stark raving mad, he took the biggest gamble of his life and informed them that, "He *was* at home – the camp was his home"; then promptly broke out in a terrified sweat in case they decided he could stay! Upon hearing this our British Medical Officer in the camp suggested to him that with all these doctors certifying he was mad he would have difficulty proving he was sane when he got home. "Don't you worry Sir", he said, "When I arrive home I'll soon show 'em I'm not barmy".

A while later six of us from the Reichbahn Party were detailed to work in an engineering works. Together with others who were already doing this job, we were marched to a factory down in Marienburg, which serviced and repaired farm implements and equipment. The other chaps had been there for some years and were quite happy, but we were distinctly unhappy, as we'd been quite content unloading coal. The regulars warned us to watch out for a particularly obnoxious lad who worked there, a boy of about seventeen who was a Hitler Youth type. We arrived, lined up and the manager came along and read out from the list, Grenville Davies, engineer. Obviously, when taken prisoner, we had been identified as having engineering experience from details in our Army pay books. Having no desire to give the Germans the advantage of our expertise we all hotly denied any knowledge of the talents they required. I denied being an engineer and told him I was a clerk, and a colleague from Coventry said he was a deep-sea diver. However, he insisted we were there to do engineering work so, as we knew all the workers had overalls, we refused to work in our uniforms and asked for overalls. It transpired that permits had to be obtained for the issue of overalls and we were informed we would receive these the next day. We told the manager that in that case *maybe* we'd work the next day. We were then delegated to 'odds and sods'. Some chaps were working outdoors, out of the main factory, and I had the job of keeping a brazier going. This became very tedious – eight hours looking after a fire! The next day we went through the same rigmarole of requesting overalls and were told we'd have them tomorrow so again we refused to work. That day, together with another chap, I was sent to work with the Hitler Youth lad. We found him taking down some overhead shafting with his ladder propped up in such a way between a beam and the shafting it showed us he had little experience of taking something down. He had looped a rope over the beam and around the shafting, and it was obvious to us that this was going to swing inwards. We were delegated to hold the rope whilst he, very arrogantly, told us what to do next. We pointedly ignored him, inviting a tirade of ranting and raving and a show of obvious delight in the responsibility of having British soldiers working for him who he could order about. Little did he know! As he was getting near the end of releasing the shaft I turned to Bill and said, "He's going to get killed". Just at that point the factory boss came past, looked to see what the lad was doing and complimented him on his work, telling him to carry on. The lad must have sensed something was going on as he noticed Bill and I were sniggering to each other. He called me over and told me to get a spanner and come up and undo a nut. I pretended not to understand so he gave the same instruction to Bill. Bill also was unable to understand his wishes at which point he became a bit flummoxed and very hesitant about what to do next. In the end I asked him if he was afraid. There was a very vehement "Nein", whereupon he gave a final turn of the bolt resulting, as we had anticipated, in the shaft swinging inwards and pinning him against his ladder. He screamed blue murder, people came running to lift it off him and he was whipped off to hospital.

On the third day we went through the same rigmarole again, no overalls so no work. I was then sent to work with another youth performing quite a trivial task dismantling shafting in a little outbuilding. He instructed me to fetch some tools and again I pretended not to understand at which point he asked what I would do. I suggested I held the ladder but he declined my offer so I told him I would look after the fire and walked away. As I did so there was an almighty crash, the ladder fell down with the youth on it and before we knew what was happening he was whipped away to hospital too. The fourth day I was detailed to work with a Polish fitter. He didn't have overalls so was working in his civilian clothes, which were covered in grease. He was a grubby little man and must have worked in the same clothes for years. He gave me a rule and instructed me to cut some pieces of metal into centimetre lengths. Once again I feigned ignorance so he took me over to where there was a mechanical saw and showed me what to do. "Undo the vice, put the metal in, lower the blade, measure it" – much to my amusement as naturally, being an engineer by trade I knew exactly what to do. Eventually he cut the piece and then instructed me to cut. I continued to insist I didn't understand how to do it until he had demonstrated the whole procedure to me about four times. At this point my face lit up and I informed him that I now understood what he was after. The saw was on runners, which contained a large weight. Instead of lowering the blade down to measure it I guessed the distance and moved the weight right to the end which made the saw come crashing down on the metal bar. Unfortunately the blade survived but the piece I managed to cut was undersize. In consequence I failed my trade test and wasn't allowed to try again. After four days of our lack of co-operation and fooling around, as well as the damage we had incurred, five of us were returned to our railway jobs.

A short while later the two shifts of Reichbahn were drafted to Maxtal, a railway rolling stock repair yard, where we were all lined up. I was a little wary when the civilian foreman of the depot passed down the line, scrutinised everybody and I was the first to be selected. As he passed on I stepped back into the ranks only to be sorted out again on his return. Together with one other I was sent off immediately to the blacksmith's shop and the rest of the party were split up to perform various tasks. There were two blacksmiths and the other fellow went to work as striker to the chargehand whilst I was appointed striker to a little Polish fellow who had been pulled out of retirement. Apparently he had been quite rotund in his working days but was now small, shrunken and wizened. His name was Stanislaus known as Stacku. He couldn't pronounce my name but very soon started calling me 'August'. At the time it didn't worry me at all, but years later, whilst reading a book about circus life I read that 'August' is the clown with the big nose and shoes; the idiot. Obviously Stanislaus was very perceptive and had summed me up to a tee. There was a smith at either end of the forge with Ludwig the chargehand at the far end being in charge of the trip-hammer, whereas at our end all the work was done by hand hammers. On Sundays we changed round and I then worked the trip-hammer. We did a variety of jobs, which proved to be most interesting. The top priority jobs sent to us were the hooks that coupled railway carriages. These frequently snapped and had to be forge-welded under the trip-hammer taking priority over all other work. Apart from Sundays, when only half the shift was working, the jobs that came in were first inspected by the chargehand who would then direct them down to my man, leaving the chargehand and his striker with nothing to do. I complained about doing all the work, which was why I was christened 'August'. Stanislaus refused to make any protest telling me it was not done, as Ludwig was the Master. However Ludwig was considerably younger than my old Stanislaus and I protested vehemently about all the work being shipped down to us. When Stanislaus set the job up I refused to work and took myself off to sit in a corner, sulk and read a book. As soon as the preparations had been made to begin the job Stanislaus called me to come and do the necessary striking but I flatly refused. As the other boys came in to get warm round the furnace he'd ask each of them to strike his metal, but they all refused too; it was quite intriguing to see how he smarmily begged and cajoled in an attempt to make the fellows work. Every now and then Stanislaus threatened to report me and I told him to do so. He'd go off in the direction of the Manager's Office. The Manager was always immaculately turned out in jackboots and riding breeches, with gold braid on his jacket. However his office was next to the toilet block and that was where Stanislaus went, but he never reported me.

Most of the boys worked in the railway sheds doing labouring work. These were big wooden sheds into which the trucks had to be shunted waiting for repair. In the early days special rations were issued for prisoners who worked long hours or did heavy work. My work was classified as heavy because of the weighty metals I had to heave about. Two civilians with astrakhan collared coats and homburg hats arrived one day doing the rounds assessing what rations we were entitled to. They came into the forge with one of our men as interpreter and the civilian foreman kept indicating in my direction. Eventually I went over and said to the interpreter, "What are they on about?" He said, "They're sorting out the rations, you're no longer entitled to heavy work rations". It didn't really matter as we all shared our rations anyway, but that was enough for me – I began objecting vociferously at the very unfairness of taking away our extra rations. The two officials became red in the face with indignation and called me a 'cheeky person' before storming out.

We worked six days a week with a skeleton staff on a Sunday and one Sunday Stanislaus had permission to have the day off to visit a relative. A fellow who worked in the carpenters' shop and who had been a smith at some time was delegated to carry out the smith's duties with me. We had been forewarned about this man when we first went to work there and were told to watch out for him, as he was an out and out Nazi and reported anything that went on. Although he was Polish he proudly sported a German forage cap decorated with red, black and white circles like the Airforce roundels. When we arrived in the morning one of the huge hooks and bar, which had snapped, was waiting to be welded. These were very long, extremely heavy objects, with wedges rammed in to hold them in position, and invariably snapped about two and a half feet from the hook. Obviously this was top priority so he began heating it and I could see immediately, as I'd now had plenty of experience welding these hooks, that it had not been heated sufficiently to do the job. I refrained from saying anything and, as I was always deputed to carry the heavy part, lifted it out when told to, putting it on the trip-hammer in order to stamp a hollow in the bar so that the hook would link in before being welded together. At this point he realised it wasn't hot enough to do the job so back into the forge it went and, to cut a long story short, this went on all day. Several times he got it too hot so that it burnt the end off and eventually reached minimum length when we then had to weld an extra piece back on. Every now and then he became so frustrated he threw things about following which he picked up an easy little job just to show he could do something. When the end of the shift came the hook and bar were still lying on the floor in three

Gwyneth Wilson, a teacher at Waseley Hills School, who attended the Congregational Church in Rubery where I was a member. During the war the church acquired names of POWs and requested female members of the congregation to correspond with them to keep up their spirits. Gwyneth, who was a Welsh girl, drew my name out of a hat and wrote to me regularly throughout the war. One evening, when she was on duty with the ARP, she asked a colleague if he would be kind enough to post her letter. He looked at it and said, "Oh, you know Grenville Davies". She said, "I've never met him in my life", to which he replied, "He's a friend of mine". He'd never had a girlfriend and I'd always regarded him as a confirmed bachelor but following this conversation they struck up a friendship and eventually married. Later they produced a son and went back to live in South Wales.

pieces. The next morning crowds of civilians were waiting in the forge and as we arrived a great cheer went up. We were totally flabbergasted but it turned out that, on his way home, the chap had thrown himself underneath a train because he couldn't bear the indignity of not having been able to do the job. He was grossly disliked and everyone agreed I'd done them a great favour by keeping quiet, thereby not having helped him to complete the task.

On another occasion a trainload of German troops came in with broken hooks on their trucks. The troops stayed in the train in the sheds overnight while repairs were carried out. When we first arrived there was one girl who worked there as a general dogsbody sweeping and generally tidying up, but later two other German girls appeared and apparently they all spent the night with the troops. To our great amusement it was rumoured afterwards that many of the troops ended up with VD, for which we secretly thanked the girls for helping the war effort.

To relieve the abject monotony I decided to act stupid and keep ducks. I found a piece of chalk and drew a pond on the forge floor. Polish civilians came to the forge to bring work and as they arrived I forbade them to go through the water shouting, "Hey, watch out – mind my ducks" – and the idiots dutifully walked round the pond rather than offend the stupid Englander. At other times I took my giraffe for a walk. I had a piece of rope with a noose on the end and walked up the yard taking my giraffe with me. Which is why, when I found out what it meant I realised how perceptive Stanislaus had been in nicknaming me 'August'.

At Maxtal, which was a very rural area, we lived in a specially erected hut on site, divided into various rooms, with a Commandant who was quite a reasonable chap. As at the main camp, apart from a small area where we played football, there was nothing to do when off duty; we were simply left to our own devices.

11

THE MARCH

The winter of 1945 was one of the coldest in modern times and Sunday, 21st January broke bitterly cold, with frost, ice, deep snow on the ground, and snowing heavily. As was usual after work, we had been reading or playing cards prior to settling down in our bunks at about 8pm. Just as we were about to settle for the night guards arrived and ushered everyone out into the corridor where we normally lined up each morning to be given our orders for the day. This time we were assembled and told to pack a haversack, take a blanket and be ready to leave in an hour. We were given no hint as to why we were leaving or where we were going. Following the usual moans, groans and bad language panic set in as during the five years of captivity everyone had collected mementoes and souvenirs to take home at the end of the war. These had no monetary value but, to each individual, became very prized personal collections. Only being allowed one haversack meant many of the possessions had to be left behind. I was fortunate; I had a rubberoid sleeping bag, which I'd bartered for a couple of years previously. Together with my mate Gordon Downie we stuffed everything we could into this using it as a kit bag. We donned as much clothing as possible, virtually two of everything, and eventually, by swapping clothes between us sorted ourselves out as best we could. I had two pairs of boots, one of which was brand new and a size bigger than the ones I was wearing, so I gave one pair to a chap who didn't possess any. Mine were a size nine or ten whereas he only took a size seven. Because of this he declined my offer at first, but being unable to find any others came back for them later when I agreed to let him have the smaller ones, and putting on extra socks to fill out the new larger ones, wore those myself. How I came to regret that decision. Brand new boots in deep snow, which was still falling heavily, meant they were extremely slippery and I kept falling down. Gordon had to constantly help me back onto my feet. Because of this I developed a very painful lump in my groin and feared I'd ruptured myself, but it was simply from where I was persistently falling, and eventually disappeared. At 9pm we were called out on parade and instructed to march. We marched to somewhere where there was a Kleinbahn (a small-gauge railway) on which we were transported a few miles eventually arriving at a large farm, which turned out to be an assembly point for all British POWs and where there were lots of other prisoners arriving from surrounding areas. Here I caught up again with Francis Hill, the lad who was captured with me, from whom I was separated in 1940 and had not seen since. He left me while we were in Stalag XXA, went to work on a farm and had been there until forced to come on this march. He looked really hale and hearty and had enjoyed his

Gordon Downie c. 1950.

work. When I'd last seen him he had dysentery, looked pale, ill and pathetic; he was a non-smoker and was very much a young boy, but he had taken up smoking during his time on the farm, had now matured and was a man. The boys on the farms became proficient at plaiting and wielding whips to herd the cattle, and Francis had very proudly brought his whip with him which he was going to take home as a memento. He was with a pal and I was with Gordon so we saw little of each other.

All through captivity, but especially from this point on through the torment of the long, soul-destroying march, it became absolutely essential to have a special friend to help you through the bad times. When at your lowest ebb and inclined to give in you supported each other, you chivvied each other along, even bullied, threatened and swore at each other at times, but you also picked each other up and helped to keep each other's spirits raised. There was no way you could give up because you would be letting your friend down if you did, and there was no way you were going to let him give up because you knew you wouldn't survive without him. When on the march I was always moaning and groaning about something but Gordon helped me along. The first time I remember taking our boots and socks off, to my horror, I saw his feet were absolutely covered in blisters, yet I never heard him moan once.

I'd always envisaged in my own mind there being far too many of we Prisoners for the Germans to be bothered with, and that at the end of the war we would be taken out to a remote place and dumped when, I assumed, they would disappear and leave us to our own devices. When we arrived at the farm I believed this was to be the case but how disillusioned one can be! We stayed for the duration of the night and early the next morning, in what we took to be the worst blizzard conditions imaginable (little did we know!), we began our long, aimless trek, the majority of our nights, with temperatures falling as low as minus twenty to minus twenty-five, spent in draughty barns. We emerged each morning unable to feel our hands and feet, stiff with cold and frozen right through. Each day as we marched we met up with yet more prisoners from other areas until there were thousands of us marching in huge columns. We kept thinking it would end the next day, but of course it didn't – just dragged interminably on and on, and we gradually began to realise that the Germans simply had no idea what to do with us other than to get us away from the Russians who were approaching from the East.

Trudging aimlessly as we were from farm to farm the only food available was potatoes. These were put into a large boiler, which had more than likely been used for pigswill, boiled and doled out – two or three potatoes each. Occasionally, joy of joys, we also received a small piece of bread.

Suddenly, and without any warning, when we came to a diversion in the road the guards decided to split us up, sending a large number of POWs in a different direction to the main column. Some weeks later the separated parties met up again and all continued to trudge along together once more as though nothing had happened. After two nights, with the weather still atrocious, Gordon and I decided we'd had enough of marching. We could hear heavy gun fire in the distance which we presumed to be the Russians, so thinking the Allies were not far away and expecting them to liberate us in the morning, under cover of darkness we slid into a ditch and waited for the column to pass. We made our way to a village and crept up into the loft of one of the wooden houses. In the pitch black it was an exceedingly eerie experience as all we could make out were the most peculiar white shapes. However, at least we were out of the cold, snow and biting winds and rested there for the night. At daybreak we discovered we were surrounded by sheets, and various other items of apparel from the family wash which, having been hung up to dry, had all frozen absolutely solid. Returning to the streets, we discovered that our hoped for rescuers were conspicuous by their absence, but a Latvian Division of the German Army was in residence. They were none too pleased to see a couple of Brits emerging from the building and while they were deciding whether to shoot us or what to do with us, I noticed outside a nearby shop a sledge, which somehow became attached to my hand and proved to be of great assistance in carrying our kit and, more importantly, a very important acquisition for carrying future supplies. Eventually the Latvians decided to escort us back to the column, which was now some distance ahead, by which time we began to realise it would be a pretty hopeless task attempting to make it on our own. There was relative safety in numbers and we stood a better chance of survival sticking together with the others. When we caught up the column was resting so we slipped quietly back into their midst and were back to square one, but this time plus a sledge. We did not receive any punishment or reprimand for our little escapade, as no one appeared to have missed us. It seemed there were so many of us, the German guards had become very disconsolate about the whole situation and no one really cared. At this stage the guards were Home-Guard types, older men who really didn't want to be involved in the war or anything to do with it. Some of them could be pretty vicious and they resented the fact that we were disrupting their lifestyle.

Gordon and I were fortunate in possessing two hundred cigarettes and a tin of tobacco which we used for bartering as we marched along, no official issue of food being received until 25th January when we were given one loaf of bread to be shared between eight of us. The following day, having covered a distance of about 22km in extremely arduous conditions, we were ushered into a school building and allowed a day of rest when we were treated to a third of a loaf each and a piece of sausage. Luxury indeed! However, at 10am the following morning we were regrouped ready to leave and to suffer what had to be our worst experience; a really horrendous day's march in even more severe raging blizzards cutting directly into our faces and bitter cold so intense that ice formed on all exposed areas of hair and flesh. Total exhaustion soon set in as every step sinking into the now deep snow proved to be a tremendous effort.

A party of Russian POWs were attached to us who were grossly undernourished – virtual skeletons – and inadequately clothed. They had been treated very roughly, their clothes were threadbare and they were a pathetic sight. By this time we had become 'worldly wise' and had been able to look after ourselves reasonably well by stealing and bartering for food to supplement the meagre rations dolled out by the Germans, but the Russians looked very bedraggled and in a terrible condition. Several of them collapsed on the way and appealed to the guards to shoot them to put them out of their misery.

Eventually we were allowed to stop and rest for a while, but just as we thought we were finished for the day the Guards got us up and, faint with fatigue, off we trudged yet again. Having been a staunch member and supporter of the church from a very early age and throughout my life it was at this point that I lost my faith completely. Conditions were so atrocious, and we were all both so mentally and physically exhausted that we could hardly drag one foot in front of the other, therefore, I could not comprehend, if there was a God, how he could possibly allow such circumstances and suffering, inflicted by man upon man, to prevail.

After many more miles we staggered into a place called Jastrow where our haven of rest was a church with the only illumination provided by a red candle glowing beneath a picture of the Madonna and Child. The remaining Russians were put on the ground floor and the British up on the balcony. The Russians smashed up furniture to light fires which gave a modicum of warmth, though the pain from slightly thawing frozen bodies and limbs was even more agonizing than the suffering already endured. Eventually silence prevailed. For some reason I shall never understand, one Russian had brought along his violin, which, through all the adversity, he still possessed. Gradually the strains of the violin began to echo around the church and the entire group of Russian Prisoners then began to chant. I had never heard the melody before, but the haunting strains of the most beautiful singing I have ever experienced in my life have remained with me to this day. (When I was going back to Poland in 2000 to retrace the steps of the march I met a Polish gentleman in Birmingham, whose daughters knew my daughter. I was recalling this experience to him and hummed the tune. Having picked out a few words when the Russians were singing in the church I called it Volga Ruski. The man sang it to me and told me it was called Volga Ruska. Several years later, and based on the same Russian folk melody, the song reached the top of the Hit Parade, sung by The Seekers and known as 'The Carnival is Over').

Gordon and I spent the night in a corner of the balcony by the organ loft and the following morning were allowed outside to relieve ourselves. Gordon stayed with our sledge on which were our soul belongings whilst I went outside to find, to my great relief, the blizzard had abated. Out in the yard I met Jimmy Dumbell from my unit who I hadn't seen since the day we were broken up in France. He had a parcel and told me there was an American Red Cross store just down the road. I dashed down to find that although all the parcels had been opened, chocolates and cigarettes had been taken while other goods were left scattered around. I grabbed a container and went round collecting up the debris, tins of meat and fats etc., in fact so much I could hardly carry it all, but in the knowledge that we had our sledge on which to transport our bounty. This, together with the cigarettes with which to barter, proved to be our salvation, for as soon as I got back into the church we were off on the march again and from then on official issues of food were extremely erratic, three or four days without rations becoming commonplace. That was one of the most amazing nights I have ever spent for it seemed that just when we were all at absolute rock bottom without prospect of improvement, totally exhausted, demoralised and when life really felt no longer worth living, food had been sent which restored my faith and helped me to believe there was a God after all.

We left the church at 8.30am and on the 29th January our only official meal consisted of one loaf to be shared between four of us. On the 30th we arrived at a German Barracks, which had been evacuated. I went scrounging around and managed to get into the canteen where I found a large enamel jug, which I filled from a barrel with its top broken open; it turned out to be cherry brandy. I also found some jam, beans and bread, and for the first time on the march we were given soup. That day we enjoyed a regular banquet!

Daily we continued the incessant, tedious marching westwards, with conditions becoming ever less bearable as food became more and more scarce. On 10th February we marched through Swienemunde, on the Baltic, which is from where the Germans were firing the V1 rockets, and later past Hanover on our way to Hamelin. Our columns were frequently split up as accommodation and feeding became more difficult. By this time the guards (who were changed at intervals) began to realise things were not going their way any longer and consequently the hardship began to tell on them as they became steadily more demoralised and we increasingly more petrified that we would eventually all be shot. As time wore on the weather improved, the constant marching became more like constant shambling as men became weaker and more ill and dysentery became ever more prevalent; but by this time no one took any notice, or cared about, the stench and filth a lot of the poor afflicted souls found themselves in and were totally unable to avoid. Otherwise nothing of any great significance happened until we got to Hamelin on 29th March. It became obvious no-one knew what to do with us so we were billeted on the outskirts of the town for several days and on 3rd April, for want of anything better to do, it was decided we would be deloused. We were split into groups and sent down to a German Barracks. My group set out in pouring rain, arrived at the barracks and had just stripped off and put our clothes in the ovens to hatch out the eggs, when allied planes appeared overhead and began bombing Hamelin. The Germans all dashed into their trenches to shelter and, much to the disgust of the Master Race, we ran out onto the parade ground stark naked to find to our great joy that quite a bit of Hamelin, including the railway station, had been blown to smithereens. We stood there in our 'birthday suits' cheering as loudly as our remaining strength would allow, and waving small pieces of hand towel with which we had been supplied to preserve our modesty! The following day we were aroused at 5.30am, taken to the remains of the station and ordered to remove bodies and clear away the debris, arriving back at the barracks at

8pm. I seemed to visualise that it had been a respectable station, but when I visited it again on my return journey in 2000 it was an exceedingly tatty old place – nothing like I remembered.

It was then decided that we would have to be moved again as it became apparent the Yanks were approaching from the westerly direction in which we had been marching. There was nothing for it but to turn us round and march back east. Again we endured daily marching until on 9th April we stopped at a farm in Schladen. Spring was fast approaching and the weather was quite pleasant. Gordon and I endeavoured to keep ourselves as clean as we were able, despite facilities not being at all conducive to hygiene. Gordon had a self-stropping razor, so when the opportunity arose we'd shave as best we could. I had the hair clippers and scissors so we cut each other's hair and kept as tidy as possible. It was while Gordon and I were shaving one day that I noticed the R.A.M.C. was holding a sick parade and who should I see but my old pal Francis Hill looking absolutely terrible. He was extremely haggard, his hair and beard were matted, he was covered in lice and filthy dirty. He told me he was dying but the medics wouldn't do anything for him. Actually there was little they could do, the only medication they possessed being aspirin. It seemed he was at his lowest ebb and had lost the will to live, so I told him to come over to me when he'd finished the sick parade and I would tidy him up a bit. Gordon and I smartened him up, cut his hair, shaved him and gave him some of our surplus clothes. Having started out with two of everything we no longer needed them all as the weather now was warmer. They were lousy as well, of course, but not as lousy as Francis'. After sprucing him up and making him look more respectable I had a word with the medics who told me that since the march began Francis had become an idle fellow who flatly refused to do anything to help himself, consequently they'd given up on him. This, sadly, was a condition many prisoners, who were totally exhausted and wasting away, succumbed to. They simply became unable to bother about themselves and even refused help that was offered to them. I explained that he was a personal friend of mine from Civvy Street who had always been fastidious about his appearance before the war and always kept himself immaculate, therefore, I felt sure he was extremely ill to have fallen into this state. I mentioned that I'd cleaned him up and begged them to do something to help him if at all possible. The medics spoke to the appropriate people who arranged for his transfer to a hospital where he remained for a further five weeks after liberation before he returned home. I didn't expect to see him again, but I heard he'd recovered and lived until the 1990s. Following his war experience he was told he would not survive if he stayed in our cold, damp climate so he went to the South of France every following winter right up until the time he died.

On 11th April we arrived at Umnendorf (from where we were liberated) where we were locked in a barn adjacent to the main road. By this time the POWs had been split so many times that our group now only numbered about two hundred. At the rear of the barn was a door, which had escaped the notice of the guards, and as it was now dark I went to look out of the rear door just as a horse and cart trundled by stacked high with crates. True to years of scrounging I grabbed a crate, which transpired to be full of cigars. Obviously the owner had been looting! We dossed down for the night and at 1am were rudely awakened from our slumbers by an English speaking civilian who announced that our guards had left, the Americans were not far away, and told us he would see we all had a good breakfast in the morning. Nobody believed him and he was showered with abuse and told in true 'Tommy' language where he should go as we wished to get as much sleep as possible. However he persisted with his story and eventually somebody did venture out, confirmed that the Guards, together with their horse and cart, had indeed gone and we were entirely on our own. In retrospect it seems incredible that nobody showed any emotion or jubilation whatsoever. I presume that by this time our general health, spirits and morale were so low that we always anticipated the worst happening and we expected the Guards would be back by morning. With this in mind we snuggled back down in the straw for a few more hours sleep. In the morning the civilian reappeared. I don't remember whether the breakfast materialised, but at 10.30 the Yanks arrived. Tanks came rumbling through and I still have a very vivid memory of the driver of the first tank, a black GI with his visor raised, smoking a large cigar. Gordon and I opened our crate and, finding it full of boxes of cigars, threw these to the Americans who reciprocated by throwing us K rations, the American equivalent of snacks, boxes containing a full meal. An officer in a jeep appeared, explained that they hadn't consolidated our area yet, advised us not to go roaming around, and told us to "Stay here until you are notified that you are safe". A couple of hours or so later the 'All Clear' came through and we were allowed out of the barn. We had a snoop around, wandered down the road and found a railway station. It was totally deserted, nobody about at all, neither civilians nor soldiers. Gordon and I found a safe, which we tried to open – all to no avail! I found a German rucksack, one of the original types made out of cowhide with the hairy part outside, which contained articles of clothing. I brought this home as a souvenir together with a book and a map, which we pinched from the station. A civilian approached, informed us there was a watchmaker's shop down the road and suggested we got him a watch, and took some for ourselves too. We wandered along and found the place, which wasn't a shop but a private house. A woman appeared looking absolutely terrified and told us the watchmaker had gone away so we entered and went into his workroom which was full of spare parts for repairs; no watches to be seen anywhere. Presumably he had taken them all with him. When we reappeared the civilian was most disgruntled and didn't believe we had found only parts of watches. The following day we were sent to get shoes from a shop in an adjacent town. I realised with hindsight how stupid I had been as there was a beautiful pair of riding boots in my size, which the shop owner wished me to have, but Gordon and I chose a pair of brown leather shoes each instead.

I think only one or two chaps sought billets in the houses in the locality the rest of us continued to doss down in the straw in the barn. There was no question of the POWs rampaging through the place, and none of us could really believe we had been liberated. We all still felt it was too good to be true and imagined we'd be back on the march again the following day.

On 14th April the Yanks took us in trucks to Hildesheim for registration from where we were each allocated a particular flight home. I was on flight seventy-one. It was strange how the number seven kept cropping up throughout my army career. My army number was 7601663, POW No. 7761, when I worked in the sugar factory I was number 71 and number 71 again for the flight home. The majority of planes were landing, loading and taking straight off. The only one on standby to wait for chaps who had gone wandering off round the local village was Gordon's, which was flight

No. 72, and which eventually flew directly back to England. I left the following morning only flying as far as Brussels, where we had a most embarrassing experience. During the evening another chap and I decided we'd have a look around the city, the magnet being a Services Club, the Montgomery Club. We entered, two dirty, scruffy, smelly, louse infested lads to find everyone else immaculately dressed, especially the Yanks whose uniforms were far superior to ours. We were so embarrassed we only stayed for about ten minutes before beating a hasty retreat.

The following morning a pile of uniforms arrived. We were all queuing up for a new uniform when the driver called, "Anyone wanting to go home jump on this truck now", upon which a great surge of lads leapt in without further ado. We were taken to Brussels Airport, boarded a plane and arrived in Wing, just outside Aylesbury at 4 o'clock that afternoon, almost five years and four months since leaving England.

We had often talked about what we would do and what we were going to have to eat when we got home. Gordon fancied a nice big, juicy steak, but I had imagined sailing, rather than flying home, and once I docked was going to have a loaf of bread, some butter and strawberry jam. This dream had kept me going through all the long tedious years of captivity and horrendous months on the march; but I never had it. When we arrived in Aylesbury we found large marquees set up and WVS people ready to feed us food galore. Stupidly we stuffed ourselves, but because of having been virtually at starvation point for five years due to the extremely meagre portions and poor quality of the majority of the food we had been able to acquire, it was too much and too rich for our stomachs to cope with and we all ended up being dreadfully ill.

Parents and relatives had been informed of our return but were told several days would elapse before we actually arrived home because of the debriefing period that was to take place. However, one officer decided that if we'd care to co-operate and give him all our details we could be debriefed within a day. Naturally we were more than happy to oblige. Then he asked if anyone had lice, and it was amazing how few of us admitted to having the infestation. Nevertheless he took us to an area where we all showered, disinfected and dusted ourselves down with DDT. Unfortunately this did not kill everything and for several months the lice remained with me, despite the fact I regularly dusted myself with DDT and pants and vests came out of lockers in a shower of the powder. The uniform I had been given that morning was taken away and we were issued with brand new kit. The following morning we were given passes and money and told we could go home. We went to Aylesbury Station feeling pretty awful as the result of the food we'd eaten. Another chap, who was unknown to me, was going to South Wales and informed me the train was due any minute. No matter, I just had to dash to the toilet telling him to catch the train and if I couldn't make it so be it. As it turned out I did make it but feeling more dead than alive. We travelled to London, crossed to Paddington and caught the train to Cardiff. As soon as we boarded I rushed to the toilet again and, returning food from both ends, felt so ill I was sure I was going to die. Having endured five years of captivity and the horrors of the interminable march the thought of dying now was unbearable. We arrived at Cardiff in the late evening too late to

Gren, together with a colleague who lived in the same road and was home on leave, cutting the cake at the VE Day celebrations.

catch a train going the nine miles to my home. I had money but didn't feel I could take a taxi for fear of throwing up in it so I lay on a bench on the platform until the first train of the morning, the milk train, left around 5am. By the time this train arrived I was feeling sufficiently improved to catch it and as it pulled in to Llanbradach Station my father, not expecting to see me for several more days, was on the opposite platform boarding a train to go to work in Cardiff. By the time he came home, being a small community, the jungle telegraph had worked and everyone knew I was home. As he stepped from the train, the Porter said the words he had been longing to hear, "Your son came home this morning".

After enduring the trauma of the march for eighty-five days with little food, only twenty rest periods and covering a distance of approximately 670 miles, mostly in atrocious conditions and all the time not knowing whether I would manage to survive or be shot at any moment, I was given three weeks leave before receiving instructions to report back to Newcastle to retrain for the Japanese war!

12

RETURN JOURNEY

In May 2000 my half-brother Anthony accompanied me on a journey to retrace the steps of my long march through Germany and Poland as a Prisoner of War. We stayed in a hotel close to where I had first been interred in Fort 17 and on the wall in the hotel foyer discovered a large map showing all the Forts (or satellite camps) up to Fort 16. Fort 17 had been the nearest Fort to the hotel in which we were staying and was close to a Railway Station, which had been clearly visible from the camp. The Railway Station, the only one in the vicinity, was still in existence, which made it very easy for me to recognise the site. Since we left the camp in 1945 a wall had been demolished on one side to widen the road, having the effect of condensing the area where the rows of barracks had once stood, and a new wall of fancy patterned concrete bricks had been constructed replacing the previous austere solid concrete blocks of the original camp wall. However, there was no indication of Fort 17 on the map, and everyone I questioned about it, including the Army Officer who eventually gave me permission to enter the complex on my return journey, all denied any knowledge of its existence. It was most bizarre and gave me a sinking feeling in the pit of my stomach. Did some dreadful atrocities occur there in the latter years of the war after we had moved on? Things local people were ashamed of and thought better to forget – who knows? When I returned home I contacted my friend Bert Deacon who confirmed I had the correct number and insisted that we *were* placed in Fort 17.

In the stables in which I was billeted some of us slept on straw on the concrete floor and others slept in tunnels, which went back into the bank like dungeons.

(27th May 2000) St. Omer where I spent my first night as a POW in 1940 in what was then the Town Hall but later became the Hotel de Ville. The building is now a tourist centre but unfortunately, when visiting it on two subsequent occasions, one when Anthony and I went on our return trip, and also when visiting with my daughters, it has been half day closing so I have been unable to enter.

During the evening of our arrival Anthony and I explored the area of the original Fort 17 camp site. The following morning I spoke to the Manager of our hotel about the Fort and the fact that I particularly remembered the tunnels. He told me he knew of a place where such tunnels still existed, and promptly took us down into the town to meet the Manager of a large car showroom, who provided us with torches and took us to the rear of his premises. He unlocked some iron gates to reveal rows of tunnels, one layer on top of another, stretching back into the hillside just like caves. Unlike ours in Fort 17, which had purely been used as sleeping accommodation, these tunnels, which presumably were originally part of another Fort, had apparently been used during the war to incarcerate

(22nd May 2000) Stalag XXA at Thorn (Now Torun) – the first POW Camp where I was interred from May to June 1940 – with wooden doors now covering the entrances to the tunnels. The wooden barracks were on the opposite side of the road.

British POWs. As we went down into the tunnels we came to a small room, which seemed to have been where a lot of the boys on serious charges had later been interred. In my time in Stalag XXA I don't remember anybody being put into solitary, this type of punishment then being very much in its infancy. It was too dark in there to enable us to take photos, but by the light of our torches we were still able to read the heart-breaking messages written on the walls. Messages for mates, from those who didn't expect to survive, to carry back to families and loved ones. One chap was going to be shot because he'd hit a German Soldier. Many had drawn cap and regimental badges. There was also a lot of vulgarity no doubt born out of the frustration, hatred, bitterness and sheer hopelessness of the situation in which they found themselves. Some of the messages were so terrible and heart rending I cannot bear to relate them. Perhaps Fort 17 had become notorious for brutality later in the war and was now best forgotten.

The following day the hotel Manager kindly asked an Army Officer from the present Polish Barracks now occupying the site of Fort 17, to escort us around them. As soon as I entered I knew I was in the correct place. The initial feeling of fear and dread I had experienced all those years ago, immediately engulfed me again and the hairs stood up on the back of my neck, as there before me, just inside the main gates, was the brick building into which I was first put as a very frightened young soldier – a three-storey brick building adorned with wooden cladding. It was like a tower, the rooms being quite small. A few of us were pushed into each of the rooms, Bert and I both being interred in the same room. We spent our first few weeks there before being moved into the stables, which were out in the main yard alongside the road, but which have long since been demolished.

(22nd May 2000) Another view of Stalag XXA – The brick buildings where no one, on my return journey, would acknowledge that Fort 17 had ever existed.

Introduction (with translation) I took with me to enable me to talk to people, and hopefully gather information, on my return trip with Anthony in 2000:

Jestesmy z Anglii. Moje nazwisko Jest Grenville Davies.
We are from England. My name is Grenville Davies.
W towarzystwie mojego brata Antoniego probuje odszukac
In the company of my brother Anthony I am trying to locate
miejsc w ktorych kiedys przebywalem jako jeniec wojenny
places in which I was a prisoner of war
w latach 1940–1945. Mowimy troche po niumiecku.
between 1940–1945. We speak a little German.
Bedziemy wdzieczni za jakakolwiek pomoc w osiagnieciu naszego celu.
We will be grateful for help in achieving our goal.

The first time I flashed these credentials around was when the Police stopped us for speeding. Anthony was driving but, as we had taken our own car, I think the driver being on the opposite side to where the police expected to see him, confused them. They dragged me out of the car and I was fined. Fortunately it was only about the equivalent of £6 but had to be paid there and then.

I was disappointed not to be able to find any landmark that reminded me where Licfett's farm had been, but everything around that area seemed to look totally different. It was now like one vast prairie so presumably had gone into communal farming with all the small fields being ploughed up. We went to Danzig where, in a bookshop, I asked the assistant if he would be kind enough to check that the name of the place as I'd known it was where the farm had been. He did so and confirmed that we had been looking in the correct place but no remaining recognisable signs existed.

When we went in search of the sugar factory we came across a little bar type place in a wooden shack where a lady was serving drinks to a few fellows. No one spoke English or German so I handed her my credentials, which she read out loud for all to hear. One of the chaps came over and when he knew what I was after decided he could speak a little German. I told him I was looking for a sugar factory and he said, "It's there". Sure

Top: (23rd May 2000) Site of POW Camp – Stalag XXB Marienburg (Malbork). The whole vast site consisted entirely of wooden buildings. I spoke to a chap who lives by the entrance who told me that when the Russians arrived in 1945 the first thing they did was burn all the wooden buildings to the ground. The only remaining bit left standing is part of one of the brick gateposts. Bottom: (23rd May 2000) Site of Stalag XXB. At the far end a civilian cemetery is now being constructed.

enough it was, right next door. We missed seeing it as over the years the hedge had grown sufficiently high for it to be obscured. It turned out he'd worked there, and realising I'd worked there as a POW insisted I must meet a colleague. He took us to a house where a young man came to the door and after explanations told us his father, who was out at that moment, had been one of the managers of the sugar factory after our time there. He invited us to return that afternoon when we met his wife, son, daughter, and father. The chap who we'd first met in the pub was also there all

Top Left: (23rd May 2000) Stalag XXB camp site overlooking the river Nogat, one of Ivanhoe Austin Gandy's attempted escape routes.
Top Right: (23rd May 2000) Anthony at the Sugar Factory at Stare Pole, Altfelde, which has been derelict since 1968.
Bottom Left & Right: (23rd May 2000) The laboratory where I worked as assistant to the chemist in 1944.

Top: (23rd May 2000) Anthony and I in Krzysztof Rybak's Garden at Stare Pole.
Bottom: (23rd May 2000) Anthony and I, together with Grandfather (who had been
Manager of the Sugar Factory) and Grandson in the garden of the Rybak Family.

Left: Maxtal (Maximilianowo) – The present owner at the old railway repair sheds. Right: Another external view of the repair sheds with train lines still in existence.

smartened up, and knowing the caretaker of the now derelict factory, had very kindly arranged for us to go inside. Whilst showing us round the fellow told us that this factory made some of the finest sugar in Poland but corruption had been rife amongst the management, which I could easily understand. The father had a magnificent, palatial house, his son also had a beautiful house in the same grounds, but the rest of the surrounding properties were very non-descript. Father admitted there were numerous fiddles taking place and in the end all the money went to certain personnel resulting in the factory dying a death.

I told him where the POWs had slept and the caretaker took us through waist high weeds to show us the spot but the only things now visible were bits of concrete in the ground.

Upon arriving at Maxtal (Maximilianowo) and having crossed a bridge, Anthony and I stopped to see whether it was a railway or river bridge. Suddenly I noticed the dirt track leading down to the old railway repair sheds, which now turned out to be a little engineering company. I spoke to the present owner who was extremely pleased to make my acquaintance and hear my story. He told us the smithy was long gone but showed us all over the factory as I pointed out all the things I remembered.

It was from these railway rolling stock repair sheds, in heavy snow and bitter cold that the March began at 9pm on Sunday, 21st January 1945.

Top Left: Interior view of the railway repair sheds at Maxtal.
Top Right: Part of the Blacksmith's Shop at the railway repair sheds.
Bottom Left: My forge was just here where I worked as Striker, and where
Stanislaus appropriately nicknamed me 'August'.
Bottom Right: When I mentioned that through the rear part I remembered using
the lathe, the owner said, "Come", opened a door and there was a lathe – a more
modern one but still in exactly the same place as the original.

When we reached the church at Jastrow in May 2000 people were entering for a service. I went round the back to see the Minister and found several choir boys many of whom understood a little English and were absolutely delighted to be able to speak English with an Englishman. One little boy offered to take me to the priest and as we set off a voice from the back bellowed, "What do you think you are doing?" Unfortunately the priest was a most unpleasant person. I asked if he could speak English,

Top Left: The church at Jastrow (Jastrowie) where I heard the Russians sing 'The Carnival is Over', the most beautiful singing I have ever heard in my life.

Top Right: Interior of the church where we sought refuge after the terrible night of blizzards – 27th January 1945. The Russian POWs slept in the nave and the British in the balcony.

Bottom Left: The corner, between the organ and the door, where Gordon and I 'dossed' down for the night.

Bottom Right: The barn at Ummendorf where we spent our last night in captivity and from where I grabbed the box of cigars from the passing horse and cart.

"No"; "Speak German?"; "No"; so I produced my credentials in which he showed no interest whatsoever and tried to push me out. I thought, "No; I've come a long way and I'm not going to be fobbed off like this", so I stood my ground and asked further questions, adding I would like to go up

Top Left: The German Barracks at Hamlin (Hamelin) to which we were taken on 29th March 1945.
Top Right: The Parade Ground at Hamlin Barracks where, during the delousing session, we ran out in our 'birthday suits' to cheer the arrival of allied planes overhead.
Bottom Left: Hamlin Station bombed 3rd April 1945 and where we were taken the following morning at 5.30am to clear the bodies and debris.
Bottom Right: Eisleben Railway Station. Gordon and I discovered this station after we had been liberated at Ummendorf on 12th April 1945. It was from here that we 'collected' the map of the area.

into the organ loft to see where Gordon and I had slept. In the end, realising I was not going to be pushed around, he detailed two senior lads who could speak English to take me there.

Record Office Stamp		**RECORD OF SERVICE**			ARMY FORM W5258

R.E.M.E. RECORDS
LEICEST

No. 4601 663 Rank CFN

Name DAVIES G .J
(in block letters)

Served in Regts/Corps as follows :

	Regt./Corps	From	To	Assn. joined with date	Remarks by Assn. (if any)
a	RAOC	28/4/39	30/9/42		
b	REME	1/10/42	9/4/46		
c					
d					

Date 21·3·46.

Record Officer

R.E.M.E

1. This card should be presented or sent by the person named above to the Regt/Corps Association he wishes to join or from which he requires assistance.
2. The Secretary of the Association should stamp and date the card in the relative column when the soldier joins the Association.
3. If you send this card by post, do not fail to enclose your address.

Wt. 40594/221 500M 1/46 KJL/1719/30 Gp. 38/3

Top Left: Graves in the British Military Cemetery at Marienburg (Marlbork) for prisoners from Stalag XXB.

Top Right: Stewart Evans and me at Digbeth bus station, Birmingham at our meeting in 2004. Stewart Evans and I were captured together by the Germans, when I was imprisoned in Poland and Stewart was imprisoned in a Camp in Bavaria. While I was in the Territorial Army Stewart was a full time soldier in the Ordnance Corps. I was Stewart's best man at his wedding in the 1940s, but after keeping in touch we lost contact with each other in the 1960s. However, following an article I wrote for our regimental magazine, which Stewart saw, he contacted me and travelled to Birmingham from his home in Cardiff to meet up with his old Army pal, 65 years after we were mobilised in Birmingham.

Bottom: My Record of Service Card.

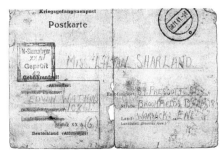

Letter cards and photo kindly lent by Barry Read. These were sent to his mother from an Edwin Watkins who, at sometime, like me, had been a POW in Stalag XXA.

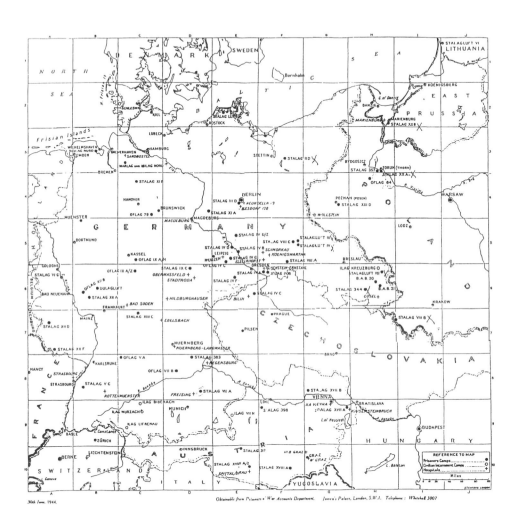

Red Cross map of Principal POW Camps in Europe.